Easy Word 6 for Windows™, Second Editon

Trudi Reisner

que

Easy Word 6 for Windows™, Second Edition

Copyright © 1994 by Que® Corporation

Library of Congress Catalog No.: 94-65888

ISBN: 1-56529-808-X

96 95 94   4 3 2

Interpretation of the printing code: the rightmost double-digit number is the year of the book's printing; the rightmost single-digit number, the number of the book's printing. For example, a printing code of 93-1 shows that the first printing of the book occurred in 1993.

Publisher: David P. Ewing

Associate Publisher: Michael Miller

Publishing Director: Don Roche, Jr.

Managing Editor: Michael Cunningham

Marketing Manager: Greg Wiegand

Credits

Publishing Director
Don Roche, Jr.

Acquisitions Editor
Thomas F. Godfrey III

Product Director
Kathie-Jo Arnoff

Production Editor
Susan Ross Moore

Technical Editor
Tish Nye

Editorial Assistants
Theresa Mathias
Jill Stanley
Michelle Williams

Book Designer
Amy Peppler-Adams

Cover Designer
Jay Corpus

Production Team
Steve Adams
Angela Bannan
Claudia Bell
Anne Dickerson
Terri Edwards
Jay Lesandrini
Elizabeth Lewis
Wendy Ott
Linda Quigley
Amy L. Steed
Michael Thomas
Lillian Yates

Indexer
Michael Hughes

Composed in *Stone Serif* and *MCP Digital* by Que Corporation.

Dedication

To Karen Giventer
with special thanks for her encouragement and support.

About the Author

Trudi Reisner is a computer consultant specializing in training users of IBM PCs, PC compatibles, and Apple Macintoshes in the use of applications software. She is the owner of Computer Training Solutions, a Boston, Massachusetts company that offers training, technical writing, curriculum development, and consulting services in software programs.

Trudi has written numerous books on Excel and other software including Que's *Allways Quick Reference*, *Ami Pro 3 Quick Reference*, *Easy 1-2-3 Release 4 for Windows*, *Easy Excel 5 for Windows*, *Excel VisiRef*, *Harvard Graphics 3 Quick Reference*, *Quattro Pro 4 Quick Reference*, and *Word for Windows 2 Quick Reference*. She is also a contributing author to *Using Ami Pro 3 for Windows*, Special Edition.

Acknowledgments

I owe thanks to many others who helped complete this book. Foremost is Kathie-Jo Arnoff, Senior Product Development Specialist at Que, for her competent skills, who reviewed the manuscript and gave suggestions and support throughout the life of this project; and Susan Ross Moore, Production Editor at Que, who managed the copy editing process for this project. Also, thanks to Don Roche, Publishing Director, who conceived the idea for this book.

Thanks to Warren Estep, who carefully reviewed the final draft. Special recognition must go to Nancy Stevenson, Acquisitions Editor at Que, who suggested the project. Special thanks to Tom Godfrey, Acquisitions Editor at Que, for his outstanding management skills, who managed the project, and whose sense of humor kept me sane throughout the life of this project.

Also, many thanks to the technical editor, Tish Nye, whose timely proofing helped maintain the accuracy of the text from cover to cover. Special thanks to the production staff who turned the final draft on disk into this printed copy in record time—a monumental task.

Finally, thanks to Microsoft Corporation, who developed and produced a fine word processing program.

Contents at a Glance

Introduction   1

Part I: The Basics   10

Part II: Entering and Editing Text   30

Part III: More Editing   64

Part IV: Managing Files   86

Part V: Formatting   102

Part VI: More Formatting   128

Part VII: Viewing and Printing the Document   188

Part VIII: Merging   202

Part IX: Sample Documents   226

Glossary   242

Index   244

Contents

Introduction   **1**

Part I: The Basics   **10**

  1   Starting and Exiting Word for Windows 14
  2   Selecting a Menu Command..16
  3   Using the Toolbar...18
  4   Hiding the Toolbar...20
  5   Hiding the Ruler...22
  6   Getting Help...24

Part II: Entering and Editing Text   **30**

  7   Adding Text..34
  8   Overwriting Text..36
  9   Moving Around the Document 38
10   Inserting a Blank Line 41
11   Combining Paragraphs 43
12   Inserting a Tab...45
13   Inserting a Page Break 47
14   Going to a Specific Page 49
15   Selecting Text 51
16   Deleting Text..54
17   Copying Text..56
18   Moving Text...59
19   Using Undo 62

Part III: More Editing — 64

20 Inserting the Date 68
21 Inserting a Special Character 71
22 Searching for Text 74
23 Replacing Text 77
24 Checking Your Spelling 81
25 Using the Thesaurus 84

Part IV: Managing Files — 86

26 Saving a Document 90
27 Closing a Document 92
28 Creating a New Document 94
29 Opening a Document 96
30 Finding a Document 98

Part V: Formatting — 102

31 Making Text Bold 106
32 Italicizing Text 108
33 Underlining Text 110
34 Changing the Font 112
35 Changing the Font Size 114
36 Centering Text 116
37 Aligning Text Flush Right 118
38 Indenting Text 120
39 Creating a Hanging Indent 122
40 Double-Spacing a Document 125

Part VI: More Formatting — 128

41 Creating a Bulleted List 132
42 Creating a Numbered List 135
43 Adding a Border to a Paragraph 138
44 Shading a Paragraph 141

45   Adding a Line to a Paragraph 144
46   Setting a Default Tab 147
47   Setting Margins 150
48   Centering a Page 152
49   Numbering Pages 155
50   Creating Headers and Footers 157
51   Editing Headers and Footers 160
52   Inserting a Graphic 162
53   Moving and Resizing a Graphic 165
54   Deleting a Graphic 168
55   Creating a Table 170
56   Entering Text in a Table 173
57   Adding a Row to a Table 176
58   Deleting a Row from a Table 178
59   Creating a Two-Column Document 181
60   Inserting a WordArt Object 184

Part VII: Viewing and Printing the Document   188

61   Displaying a Document in Page Layout View 192
62   Zooming a Document 194
63   Previewing a Document 197
64   Printing the Document 199

Part VIII: Merging   202

65   Creating a Main Document 206
66   Creating a Data Source 208
67   Saving the Data Source 212
68   Entering Records into the Data Source 214
69   Typing the Main Document 217
70   Saving the Main Document 221
71   Merging the Files 223

Part IX: Sample Documents — 226

Create a Memo 228
Create a Business Letter...230
Create a Report..232
Create a Resume 234
Create a Newsletter 236
Create an Invitation...238
Create a Contract 240

Glossary — 242

Index — 244

Introduction

TKO Toys
Sales Report

Executive Summary

Sales increased 15% this year.

Five new products were introduced.

Operating costs continued to rise, with a 8% increase this year.

Division Sales

The following table shows a breakdown of sales by division. As you can see, the East and North divisions continued to dominate sales. The fourth quarter increase can be attributed to the introduction of three new products that quarter.

	1st Quarter	2nd Quarter	3rd Quarter	4th Quarter
East	120,000	150,000	135,000	225,000
West	80,000	90,000	85,000	160,000
North	100,000	125,000	135,000	200
South	70,000	60,000	60,000	120

New Products

The following new products were released this year:

Dinosaur Robots
Queenie Dolls
Little Miss Twinkle Toys
Terror Trolls

Sales Report

Nancy Tumarkin
150 Grapevine Road
Beverly Farms, MA 01916

EDUCATION

Master of Business Administration, Boston University, Boston, Massachusetts.

Bachelor of Science degree in communications, Boston University, Boston, Massachusetts. Graduated magna cum laude.

EXPERIENCE

Vice President of Marketing, MRO Corporation.
- Manage staff of 30 public relations specialists, copy writers, and product designers.
- Coordinate and plan all marketing pieces: catalogs, promotional pieces, direct mail.
- Responsible for look and design of all company products.
- Responsible for budget of 1.2 million.

Director of New Products, MRO Corporation.
- Design and suggest new product lines.
- Work with product designers and engineers to ensure quality product.
- Coordinate product testing and product launches.
- Developed and launched 3 new product lines during tenure.
- New product lines generated 3.5 million in net revenue.

Advertising Director, S&O Advertising.
- Managed 15 account representatives, ensuring all clients received quality work. Directly worked for the top 2 accounts, designing and coordinating advertising campaigns.
- Solicited new clients.
- Added 7 new clients.

Managing Editor, Boston 128 News
- Manage staff of 20 writers, editors, and page layout.
- Direct editorial staff on selecting articles and feature stories
- Coordinate printing and production process.
- Circulation grew 15% during tenure as managing editor.

REFERENCES

Available upon request.

Volume 11

Broad Ripple News

Spring 1994

Butterfly Collection

Famed butterfly collector, Jerome Hanley, will be in Broad Ripple this weekend to display his collection of over 250 butterflies. Mr. Hanley has been to every continent, 50 different countries in his quest for the ultimate butterfly collection.

The collection will be on display in Hanley's Art Gallery from 10AM to 5PM all next week.

New Store Opens

Welcome to Broad Ripple Village the new shop Polka Dots. This new children's clothing store is open 10AM to 6PM., Monday through Saturday and feat   gh finest child   f the

As a grand opening special, all merchandise will be 20% off for the month of March.

Annual Spring Fair

The Broad Ripple Spring Fair is scheduled for April 4 at the Broad Ripple Park. Art booths, food, and entertainment all make the fair the place to be.

This year over 50 local artists will be displaying their work. Some artists will be providing demonstrations and discussing artistic techniques.

Entertainment will be provided by the Spinsations, a local band. Also, clowns, jugglers, and storytellers will be around to delight the children attending.

Look for Joe and Ann's BBQ tent. Other local restaurants will provide tasty treats and refreshing drinks.

Cost of admission is $14; children under 12 are free. For more information on the Fair, call Susan Corazato at 555-9011.

Inside...

Welcome new BRVA President
Renovation Plans for Park Valuable
Coupons

Join us for a Wine Tasting Party!

WHEN: *Saturday, December 16*
      8PM to 11PM

WHERE: *6423 North Beacon*

RSVP: *Kathleen Gill*
      555-0911

What You Can Do with Word

Microsoft Word for Windows is one of the world's most popular word processing software programs. You could create the documents on a typewriter, but Word makes writing, editing, and printing easier.

Specifically, you can use Word to perform these functions:

- *Correct errors.* With a typewriter, after you press a key, that letter is committed to paper. To correct a mistake, you have to use correctors such as *Whiteout* or retype the document. With Word, you see the text on-screen. You can easily correct any typographical errors before you print the document.

- *Move around quickly.* With the document on-screen, you can move from one sentence, paragraph, or page to another. You can move quickly from the top of the document to the bottom and vice versa.

- *Make editing changes.* You can insert text into any location in your document. You also can delete any amount of text quickly, such as a character, a word, a sentence, a paragraph, or a block of text.

- *Rearrange your text.* When you sit down to write, you don't always write in order from the introduction to the summary. Ideas may occur to you in a different order. As you're writing the summary, you might think of an idea that belongs in the introduction. With Word, you can easily move and copy text from one location to another.

- *Restore deleted text.* When you accidentally delete text that you want to keep, you don't have to retype it. Instead, you can just restore the text.

- *Check spelling.* Before you print, you can run a spell check to search for misspellings and double words. If you are a poor typist, this feature enables you to concentrate on your writing and leave spelling errors for Word to catch.

■ *Search for text.* You can search your document for a particular word or phrase. For example, you can move quickly to the section of your document that discusses expenditures by searching for the word *expenditures*.

■ *Search and replace text.* You can make text replacements throughout the document quickly and easily. For example, you can change all occurrences of the name *Smith* to *Smythe* in a document.

■ *Make formatting changes.* Word enables you to easily change margins, tabs, and other formatting options. You can experiment with the settings until the document appears the way that you want it. Then you can print it.

■ *Change how text is printed.* You can boldface, italicize, and underline text. Word also lets you shade paragraphs and add borders. You also can use a different typeface, depending on your printer.

■ *Preview your document.* You can preview your document to see how it will look when you print it. If you want to make changes before you print, you can do this when you return to normal view.

■ *Add bulleted lists.* Add bullets to your document to emphasize text. Word has supplied a range of bullets depending upon your preference or needs.

■ *Add borders.* Borders can be added to any text, paragraph, or document. Borders can be created in a variety of widths, from thin to thick. There is also a 3-D effect available for adding special effects.

■ *Create headers and footers.* Word offers the capability to create custom headers and footers for your documents, or you may choose from the standard selections that are offered.

■ *Import data or graphics into your document.* You can import graphics or data from other applications into your document.

Introduction

Task Sections

The Task sections include numbered steps that tell you how to accomplish certain tasks, such as saving a document or indenting a paragraph. The numbered steps walk you through a specific example so that you can learn the task by actually doing it.

Big Screen

At the beginning of each task is a large screen shot that shows how the computer screen will look after you complete the procedure that follows in that task. Sometimes the screen shot shows a feature discussed in that task, however, such as the Go To dialog box.

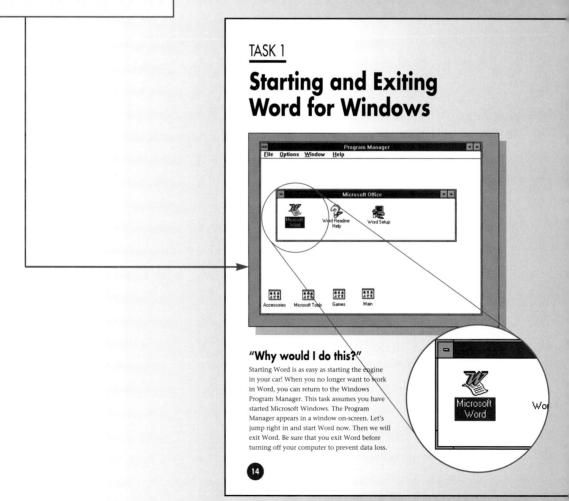

TASK 1

Starting and Exiting Word for Windows

"Why would I do this?"

Starting Word is as easy as starting the engine in your car! When you no longer want to work in Word, you can return to the Windows Program Manager. This task assumes you have started Microsoft Windows. The Program Manager appears in a window on-screen. Let's jump right in and start Word now. Then we will exit Word. Be sure that you exit Word before turning off your computer to prevent data loss.

14

Step-by-Step Screens

Each task includes a screen shot for each step of a procedure. The screen shot shows how the computer screen looks at each step in the process.

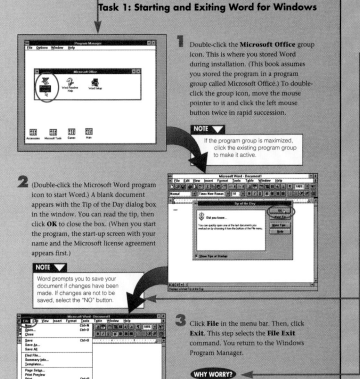

Task 1: Starting and Exiting Word for Windows

1 Double-click the **Microsoft Office** group icon. This is where you stored Word during installation. (This book assumes you stored the program in a program group called Microsoft Office.) To double-click the group icon, move the mouse pointer to it and click the left mouse button twice in rapid succession.

NOTE ▼
If the program group is maximized, click the existing program group to make it active.

2 (Double-click the Microsoft Word program icon to start Word.) A blank document appears with the Tip of the Day dialog box in the window. You can read the tip, then click **OK** to close the box. (When you start the program, the start-up screen with your name and the Microsoft license agreement appears first.)

NOTE ▼
Word prompts you to save your document if changes have been made. If changes are not to be saved, select the "NO" button.

3 Click **File** in the menu bar. Then, click **Exit**. This step selects the **File Exit** command. You return to the Windows Program Manager.

WHY WORRY?
When you're using the mouse to execute a command, make sure you double-click the left mouse button. If nothing happens, check the location of the mouse pointer and try double-clicking again.

15

Why Worry? Notes

You may find that you performed a task, such as sorting text, that you didn't want to do after all. The Why Worry? notes tell you how to undo certain procedures or get out of a situation, such as by displaying a Help screen.

Other Notes

Many tasks include other short notes that tell you a little more about certain procedures. These notes define terms, explain other options, refer you to other sections when applicable, and so on.

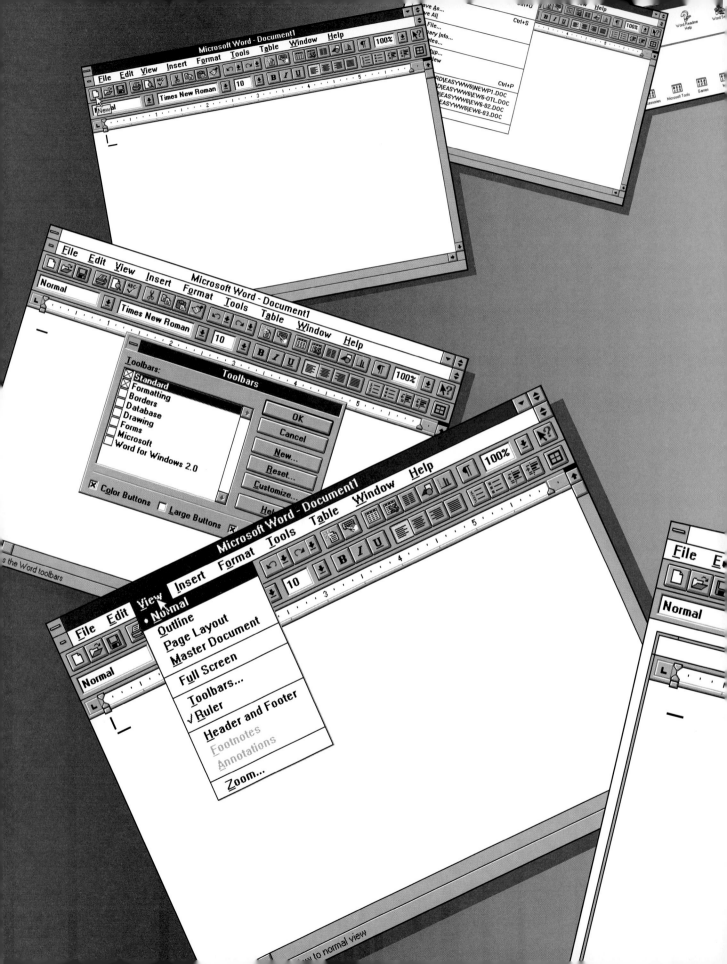

PART I
The Basics

1 Starting and Exiting Word for Windows

2 Selecting a Menu Command

3 Using the Toolbar

4 Hiding the Toolbar

5 Hiding the Ruler

6 Getting Help

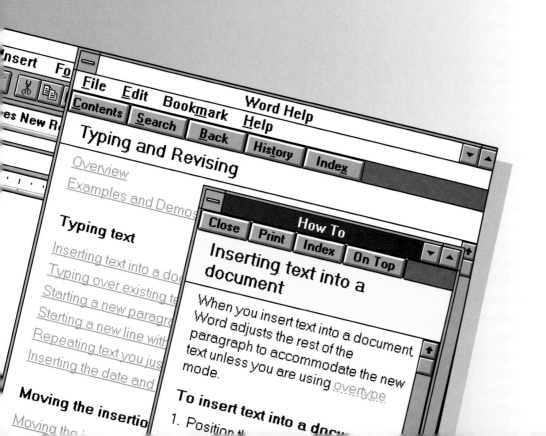

Part I of this book introduces you to Word basics. You need to know some fundamental things about Word before you start creating your own documents.

In this part, you will learn how to start and exit Word. You should ensure that Word is installed on your hard disk so that it appears in your Windows Program Manager as a program icon. For installation instructions, refer to your Microsoft Word version 6 for Windows documentation. You can start and exit Word as you would any Windows application.

When you start the program, Word displays a blank document—much like a blank piece of paper. The document is a file in which you store your data.

The *menu bar* is just below the title bar at the top of the screen. This line displays the main menu names. In this part, you learn how to select a menu command. If you prefer to keep your hands on the keyboard, learn the shortcut keys that appear in the menus next to the command names. This book notes some shortcut keys in the exercises.

When you choose a command followed by (...), Word displays a *dialog box*. The dialog box prompts you for additional information. Some dialog boxes have more than one set of options. This is indicated by the folder tabs at the top of the dialog box. You can display the other set of options by clicking on the tab.

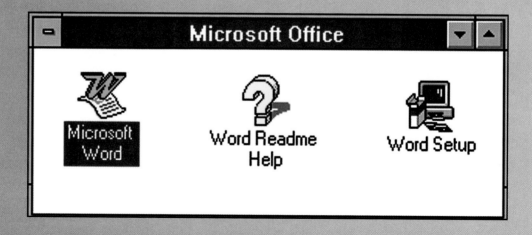

The *toolbar* that appears below the menu bar provides quick access to commands that you use frequently. Word ships with many different toolbars that include the tools you use for formatting a document, drawing graphics in the document, creating macros, and many other Word operations. Word also offers the ability to create new toolbars or modifying existing toolbars.

The Standard toolbar, the Formatting toolbar, and the ruler appear when you start Word. Sometimes you might want to have a clean screen, or you may want to make more lines of text in a document visible. You can hide the toolbars and the ruler to make more room on-screen.

In this part, you are shown how to view ToolTips (the toolbar button names). Word's new ToolTips feature displays the button names for each button on the toolbar as well as a description of the button in the status bar.

The *insertion point* is a flashing vertical bar that appears in the document window. Text that you type appears at the position of the insertion point.

This part also discusses some of the ways you can get help in Word. You can get instant on-line Help, look at the Quick Preview, Examples and Demos, and view the tip of the day. Word's Tip of the Day feature has tips for many Word operations.

The tasks that follow in this part teach essential skills that you will need to perform many of Word's operations.

TASK 1

Starting and Exiting Word for Windows

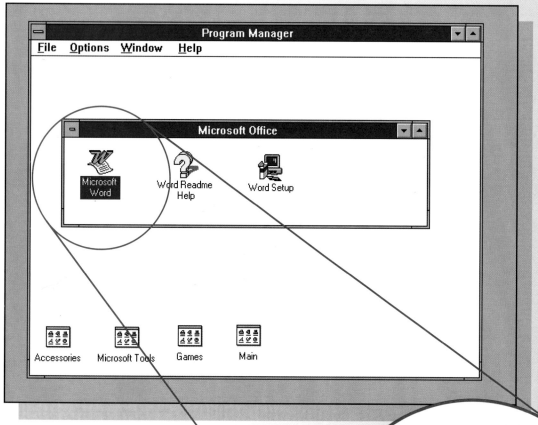

"Why would I do this?"

Starting Word is as easy as starting the engine in your car! When you no longer want to work in Word, you can return to the Windows Program Manager. This task assumes you have started Microsoft Windows. The Program Manager appears in a window on-screen. Let's jump right in and start Word now. Then we will exit Word. Be sure that you exit Word before turning off your computer to prevent data loss.

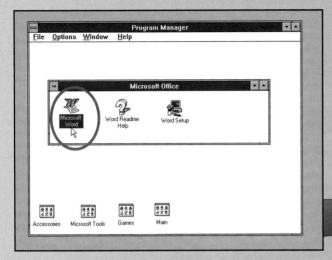

1 Double-click the **Microsoft Office** group icon. This is where you stored Word during installation. (This book assumes you stored the program in a program group called Microsoft Office.) To double-click the group icon, move the mouse pointer to it and click the left mouse button twice in rapid succession.

NOTE ▼

If the program group is maximized, click the existing program group to make it active.

2 (Double-click the Microsoft Word program icon to start Word.) A blank document appears with the Tip of the Day dialog box in the window. You can read the tip, then click **OK** to close the box. (When you start the program, the start-up screen with your name and the Microsoft license agreement appears first.)

NOTE ▼

Word prompts you to save your document if changes have been made. If changes are not to be saved, select the "NO" button.

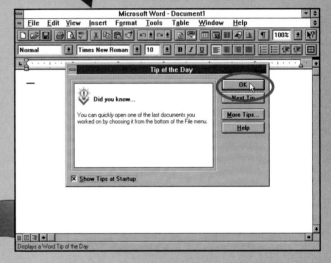

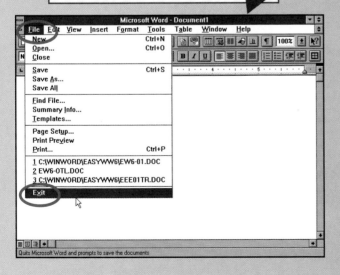

3 Click **File** in the menu bar. Then, click **Exit**. This step selects the **File Exit** command. You return to the Windows Program Manager.

WHY WORRY?

When you're using the mouse to execute a command, make sure you double-click the left mouse button. If nothing happens, check the location of the mouse pointer and try double-clicking again.

TASK 2
Selecting a Menu Command

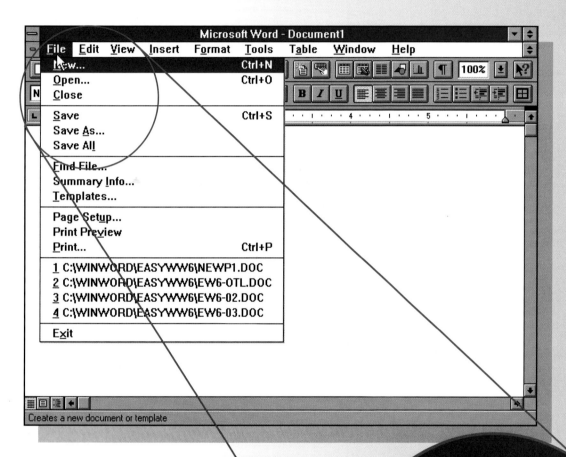

"Why would I do this?"

Word's menu bar is located directly below Word's application title bar. This menu bar contains pull-down menus for Word commands. The toolbar menu can also be used to execute the same commands shown in the menu bar.

Let's examine how to select a menu command.

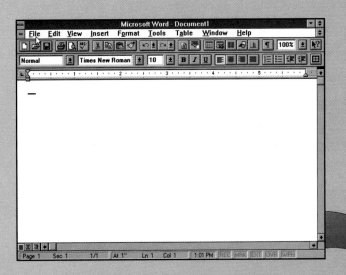

1 Start Word. If you need help with this step, see *"Task 1: Starting and Exiting Word for Windows."*

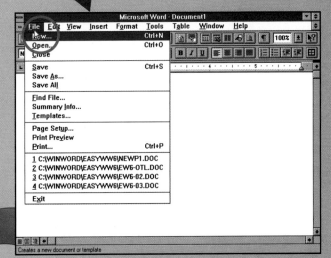

2 Point to **File** in the menu bar and click the left mouse button. This step opens the menu. In this case, you are opening the File menu. You see a list of File commands.

3 Point to **Exit** and click the left mouse button. This step selects the command. In this case, you are selecting the Exit command. You return to Microsoft Windows Program Manager.

WHY WORRY?

To close a menu without making a selection, click the menu name again or press Esc.

Using the Toolbar

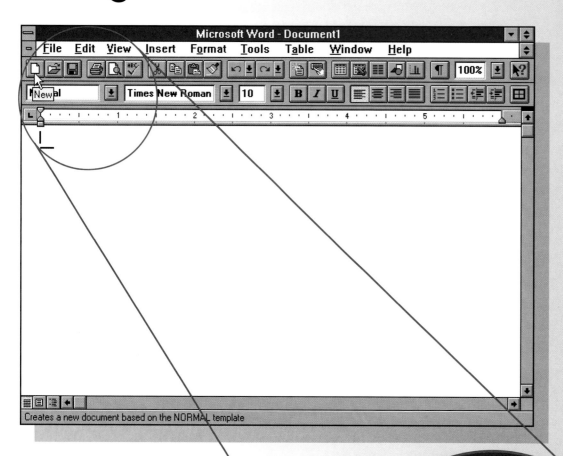

"Why would I do this?"

The Standard toolbar contains buttons for common Word commands. The Formatting toolbar contains lists and buttons for common formatting commands. You need a mouse to use the toolbars. To perform tasks quickly, select a toolbar button rather than a menu command. When you leave the mouse pointer on a toolbar button, Word displays its name near it. A description of the button also appears in the status bar at the bottom of the screen. Let's view the name of the first button on the Standard toolbar and then select it.

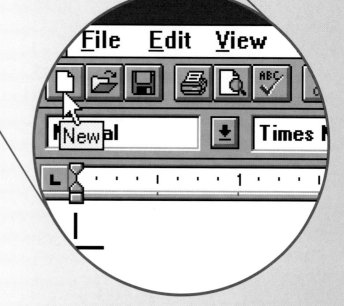

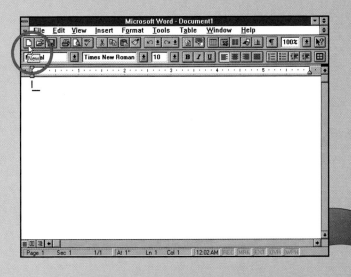

1 Point to the **New** button, the first button from the left on the Standard toolbar, and leave the mouse pointer on the button. This step displays the button's name, New, in a yellow box near the button. This is the ToolTip feature.

WHY WORRY?

Be sure to move the mouse pointer directly over the toolbar button. If the ToolTip does not appear, try moving the mouse pointer again and pause a few seconds.

2 Click the **New** button. Word opens a new document and displays DOCUMENT2 on top of DOCUMENT1. Click **File** in the menu bar. Then click **Close**. Word closes DOCUMENT2.

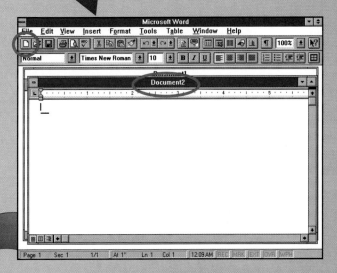

3 DOCUMENT1 is now the active document.

TASK 4
Hiding the Toolbar

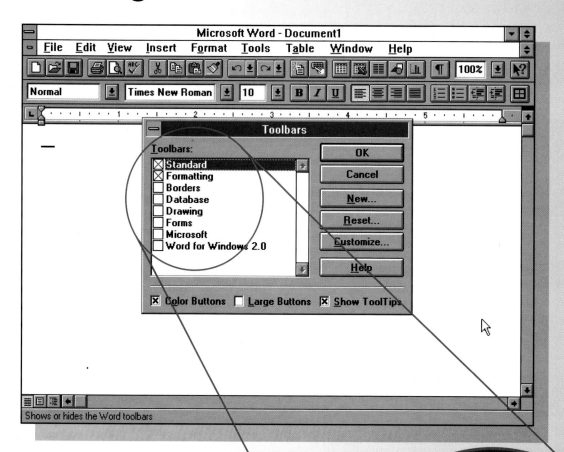

"Why would I do this?"

By default, the Standard toolbar and Formatting toolbar appear at the top of the screen. But, perhaps you want to have a clean screen, or you may want to make more lines of text in a document visible. You can hide the toolbars to make more room on-screen.

Let's hide the Standard toolbar.

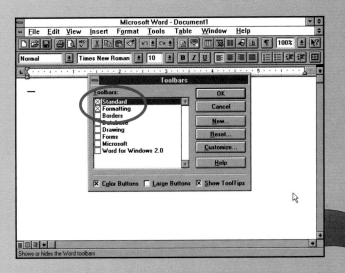

1 Point to **View** in the menu bar and click the left mouse button. Then, point to **Toolbars** and click the left mouse button. This step selects the View Toolbars command. You see the Toolbars dialog box, which lists the toolbars. An "X" next to the toolbar name indicates that the toolbar is displayed.

2 Click the box next to the Standard option. When the option is selected, an "X" will appear. Clicking again on the box removes the "X" and tells Word not to display the Standard toolbar. Click **OK**.

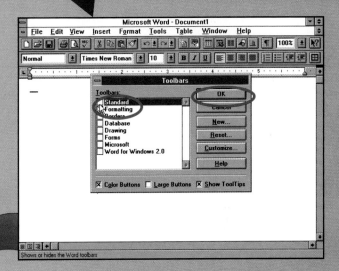

3 The Standard toolbar is hidden.

WHY WORRY?

Follow the same steps to display the toolbar. To display the toolbar, make sure that there is an "X" in the check box next to the toolbar name.

TASK 5
Hiding the Ruler

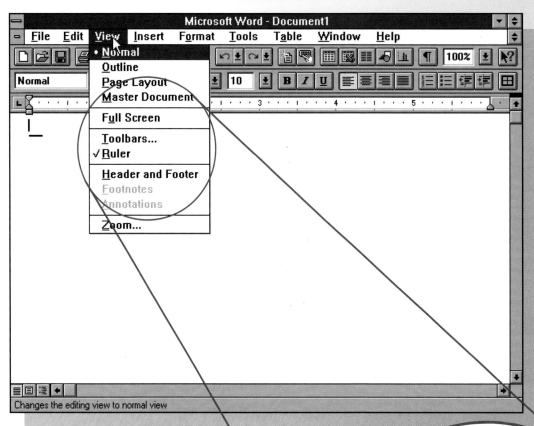

"Why would I do this?"

By default, the ruler appears beneath the
Formatting toolbar. You can use the ruler to
change tabs and margins quickly. However, you
might want to have a clean screen, or you may
want to make more lines of text in a document
visible. You can hide the ruler to make more
room on-screen. For beginners, the screen may
be less confusing with the ruler hidden.

Let's hide the ruler.

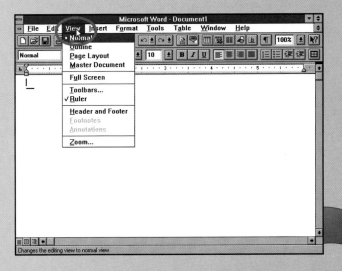

1 Point to **View** in the menu bar and click the left mouse button. This step opens the View menu. You see a list of View commands.

2 Point to **Ruler** and click the left mouse button. This step selects the Ruler command. The ruler is hidden.

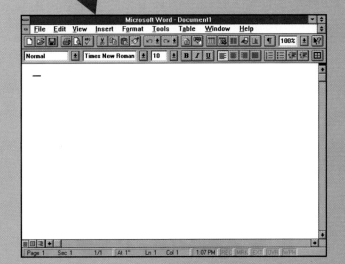

NOTE ▼

If you select this command when the ruler is displayed on-screen, Word hides the ruler. If you select this command when the ruler is hidden, Word displays the ruler.

WHY WORRY?

The Ruler command is a toggle. Select the Ruler command again to display the ruler.

TASK 6
Getting Help

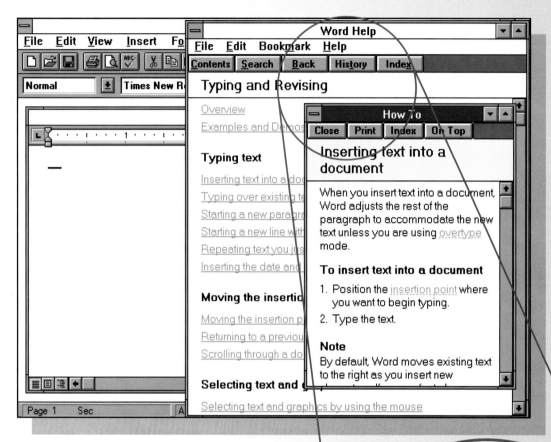

"Why would I do this?"

Word offers many ways to get help, and the Help feature has its own menu system. Word's new Tip of the Day feature shows you a few of the many shortcuts in Word.

First, let's get some help on how to insert text. Then, we will use the Tip of the Day to learn about Word's many shortcuts.

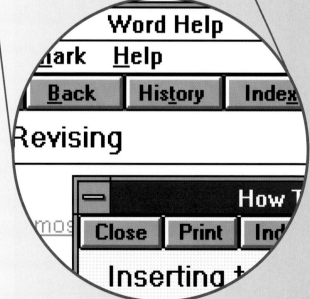

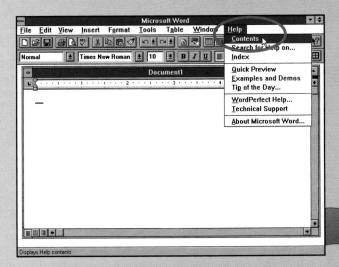

1 Click **Help** on the menu bar. Then click **Contents**. This step selects the Help Contents command. Word opens the Help window. The name of the Help window appears on the title bar. You see a list of Help topics.

NOTE ▼

You can also click the Help button in a dialog box to get help on the command for which you are setting options.

2 Point to the topic **Using Word** and click the left mouse button. This step selects the Help topic and displays a list of topics.

NOTE ▼

When the mouse pointer is on a topic for which you can get help, the pointer changes to a hand with a pointing finger.

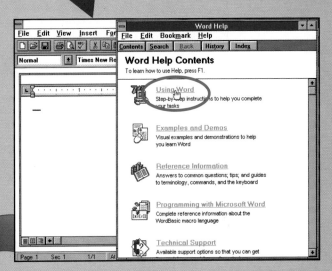

3 Point to the topic **Typing and Revising** and click the left mouse button. This step selects the Help topic and displays a list of subtopics.

Task 6: Getting Help

4 Point to the topic **Inserting text into a document** and click the left mouse button. This step selects the Help topic and opens the How To dialog box. This dialog box contains the steps you follow to insert text into a document.

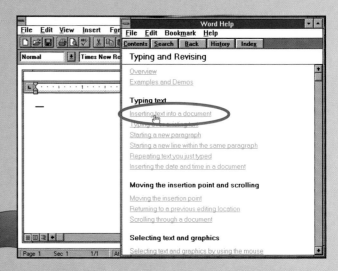

5 Click the **Close** button in the How To dialog box. Word closes the How To dialog box.

6 Click **File** on the Help window's menu bar. Then, click **Exit**. This step selects the Exit command and then closes the Help window.

WHY WORRY?

To shut the Word help window quickly, double-click the Control menu box. This box is the small bar to the left of the window's title bar.

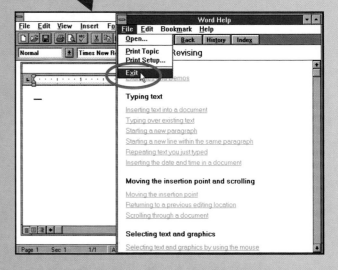

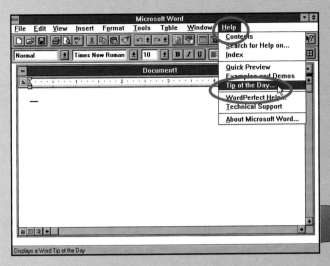

7 Click **Help** on the menu bar. Then, click **Tip of the Day**. This step selects the Help Tip of the Day. Word then displays one of Word's shortcuts.

NOTE ▼

The Tip of the Day appears when you start Word so you can learn Word's many shortcuts. If you do not want the Tip of the Day to appear each time you start Word, deselect the *Show Tips at Startup* check box located at the bottom left of the dialog box.

8 Click the **Next Tip** button. Word displays the next tip in the Did you know box.

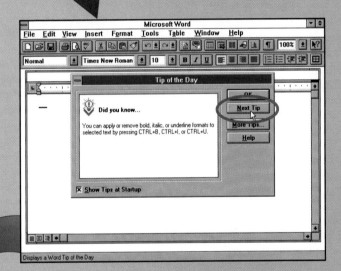

9 Click the **More Tips** button. Word displays the Tip index in Word's Help window.

10 Point to the topic **Copying and moving text,** and click the left mouse button. This step selects the Tip topic and displays a list of shortcuts for copying and moving text.

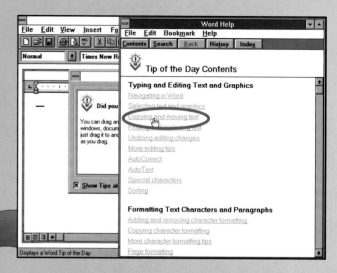

11 Click **File** in the Help window's menu bar. Then, click **Exit**. This step selects the Exit command, and then closes the Help window.

12 Click **OK**. This step closes the Tip of the Day dialog box.

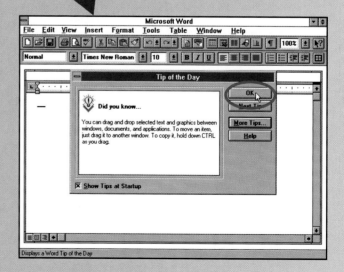

PART II

Entering and Editing Text

7 Adding Text

8 Overwriting Text

9 Moving Around the Document

10 Inserting a Blank Line

11 Combining Paragraphs

12 Inserting a Tab

13 Inserting a Page Break

14 Going to a Specific Page

15 Selecting Text

16 Deleting Text

17 Copying Text

18 Moving Text

19 Using Undo

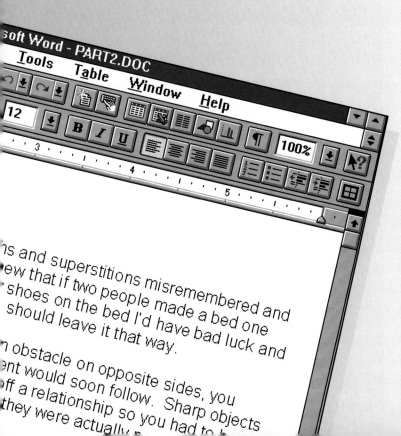

Part II: Entering and Editing Text

Any time you open up an existing document to continue work on it, you're adding to it. You can use some simple editing features to add text to an existing document. These features include Insert mode and Overtype mode. This part discusses both modes for adding text.

To add text to any document, you can either type in new text, or cut and paste text from another document. It is even possible to merge another text file with the current one (it's called Inserting a file).

The document is often much larger than one screen can possibly display at one time. To place text in other areas of the document, you must be able to move to the desired locations. There are many ways to move around the document. You can use the arrow keys to move one character at a time. You can also use key combinations to quickly move around the document.

With Word for Windows' Go To command you can jump to a specific page that is out of view.

You can navigate around the document with the following arrow keys and key combinations:

To move	Press
Right one character	→
Left one character	←
Up one line	↑
Down one line	↓
To the previous word	**Ctrl+←**
To the next word	**Ctrl+→**
To the beginning of a line	**Home**
To the end of a line	**End**
To the beginning of the document	**Ctrl+Home**
To the end of the document	**Ctrl+End**
To the previous screen	**PgUp**
To the next screen	**PgDn**

In this part, we will also show you how to move quickly around the document with the mouse.

After you enter data, you can overwrite text, insert a blank line, combine paragraphs, insert a tab, and insert page breaks.

This part also shows you how to select, or highlight text, defining a portion of text that you want to overtype, delete, move, copy, edit, or enhance. Word for Windows highlights text you select.

You can select text with the following key combinations:

To select	Press
One character to the right of the insertion point	**Shift**+→
One character to the left of the insertion point	**Shift**+←
One line above the insertion point	**Shift**+↑
One line below the insertion point	**Shift**+↓
From the insertion point to the end of the line	**Shift**+**End**
From the insertion point to the beginning of the line	**Shift**+**Home**

To deselect text by using the keyboard, press any of the respective arrow keys.

In this part, we will also show you how to select text quickly with the mouse.

In this part, you also learn how to delete text, copy text, move text to other locations in the document, and undo mistakes.

TASK 7
Adding Text

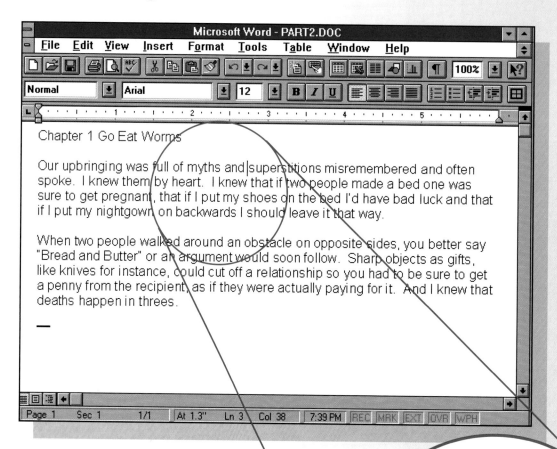

"Why would I do this?"

Normally, Word is in Insert mode. In Insert mode, you type text at the insertion point and the existing text moves forward to make room for the new text. In Word for Windows, you may find that you need to change a document by adding or replacing text after the document is complete.

In the following task, you will enter text for the first chapter of a document. Then you will insert additional text.

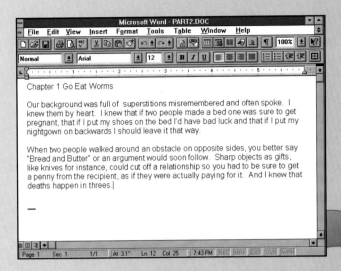

1 Type the text that appears in the figure so that your computer screen matches the screen in the book. This step enters the text for the document.

WHY WORRY?

If you make a mistake when typing text, use the Backspace key or Delete key to correct the entry.

2 Click before the word *superstitions*. This step places the insertion point where you want to insert text. You can place the insertion point by clicking the location or by using the arrow keys.

NOTE ▼

Do not press the Insert key to insert text. Pressing the Insert key puts Word for Windows in Overwrite mode. See the next task, *Task 8: Overwriting Text*.

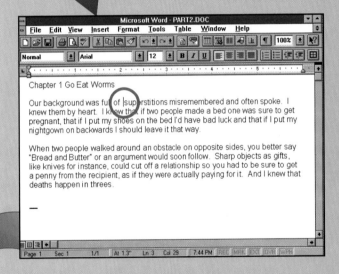

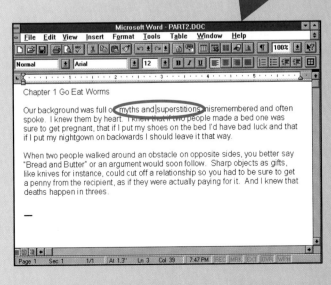

3 Type **myths and**. Then, press the **space bar**. This step inserts the new text and shifts the existing text to the right with a space between the new text and the original text.

WHY WORRY?

To delete the text, click the Undo button on the Standard toolbar immediately after typing the new text. Or, simply delete the text. *See Task 16: Deleting Text*.

TASK 8
Overwriting Text

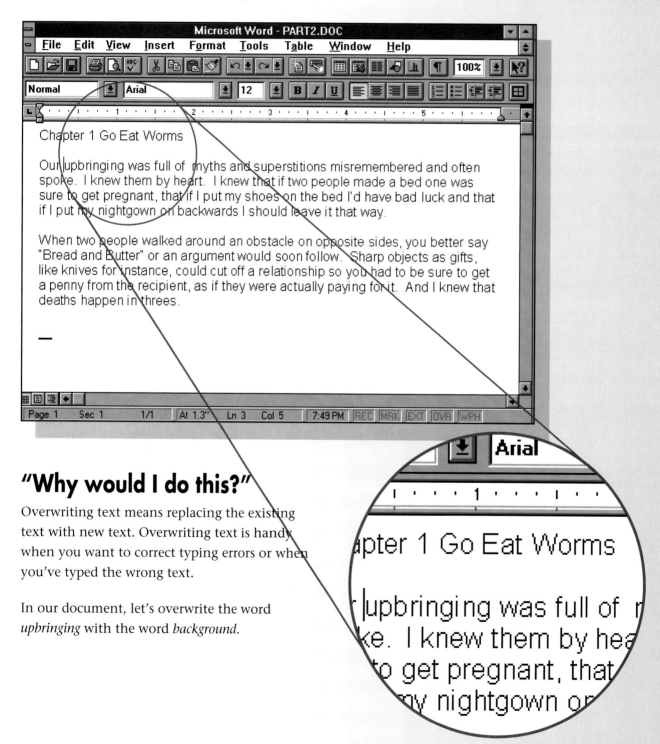

"Why would I do this?"

Overwriting text means replacing the existing text with new text. Overwriting text is handy when you want to correct typing errors or when you've typed the wrong text.

In our document, let's overwrite the word *upbringing* with the word *background*.

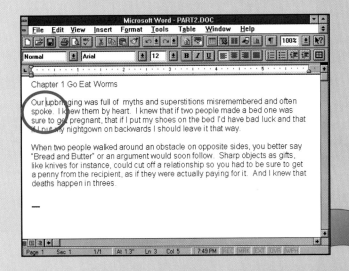

1 Click before the *u* in *upbringing*. This step places the insertion point where you want to overwrite text. You can place the insertion point by clicking the location or by using the arrow keys.

2 Press **Insert**. This step puts Word for Windows in Overwrite mode. The indicator OVR appears in the status bar at the bottom of the screen. This mode overwrites rather than inserts text.

NOTE ▼

You can also select the text you want to replace and start typing. The new text replaces all the selected text.

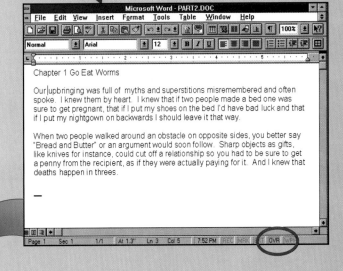

3 Type **background**. Word for Windows deletes the original text and replaces it with *background*. Then, press **Insert**. The Insert key is a toggle. You press this key one time to turn on Overwrite mode. You press it again to turn off Overwrite mode.

WHY WORRY?

To reverse the change, follow the same steps. You cannot undo overwritten text.

Moving Around the Document

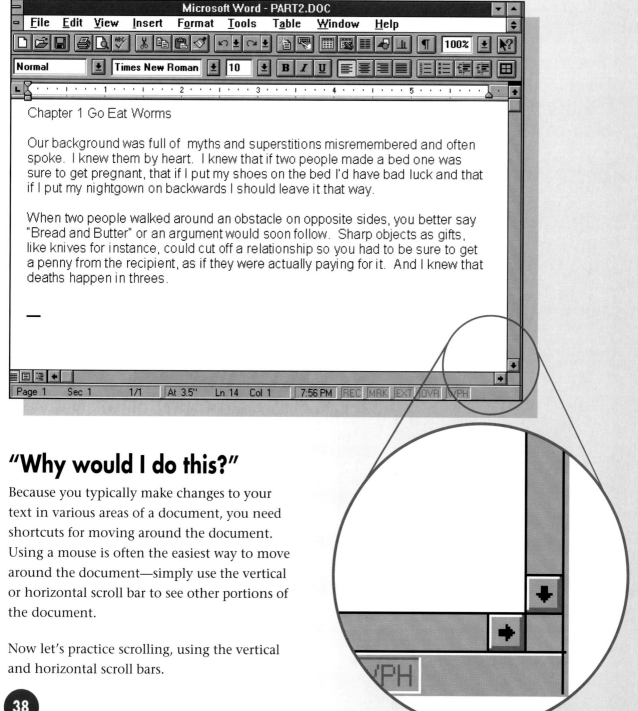

"Why would I do this?"

Because you typically make changes to your text in various areas of a document, you need shortcuts for moving around the document. Using a mouse is often the easiest way to move around the document—simply use the vertical or horizontal scroll bar to see other portions of the document.

Now let's practice scrolling, using the vertical and horizontal scroll bars.

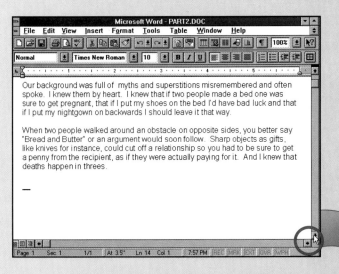

1 Click twice on the down scroll arrow at the bottom of the vertical scroll bar. Clicking the down scroll arrow moves the document down one or more lines at a time, depending on the length of the document.

NOTE ▼

You can point to the up, down, left, or right scroll bar arrow and hold down the mouse button to scroll the document continuously in a particular direction.

2 Click three times on the up scroll arrow at the top of the vertical scroll bar. Clicking the up scroll arrow scrolls the document up one or more lines at a time, depending on the length of the document.

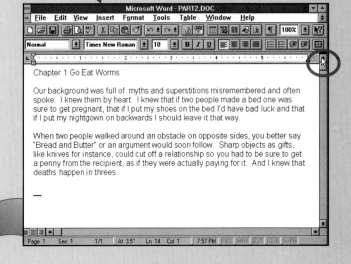

3 Click halfway down in the vertical scroll bar itself. Clicking in the scroll bar moves the document up or down one window length at a time. Notice that the scroll box is one-quarter of the way down the vertical scroll bar.

Task 9: Moving Around The Document

4 Drag the scroll box up to the top of the vertical scroll bar. Dragging the scroll box moves the document quickly to a new location in the direction of the scroll box. In this case, Word for Windows moves the document up to the top of the screen and displays the beginning of the document.

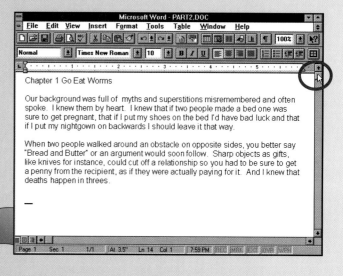

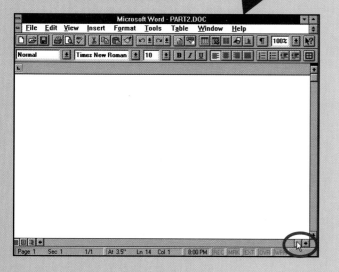

5 Drag the scroll box to the far right of the horizontal scroll bar. Dragging the scroll box moves the document quickly to a new location in the direction of the scroll box. In this case, Word for Windows moves the document to the far left of the screen and displays the right side of the document.

NOTE ▼

Keep in mind that whatever scroll bar action you perform on a vertical scroll bar can be performed the same way on the horizontal scroll bar. If you click on a horizontal scroll arrow, Word for Windows moves the document left or right by a few characters. If you click on the scroll bar, Word for Windows moves the document right or left by one window width. Dragging the horizontal scroll box moves the document left or right, depending on where you reposition the scroll box.

WHY WORRY?

If you run out of room to move the mouse on your desktop or mouse pad, just lift the mouse and then put it down. The mouse pointer will not move when the mouse is in the air. Then try moving the mouse again.

TASK 10

Inserting a Blank Line

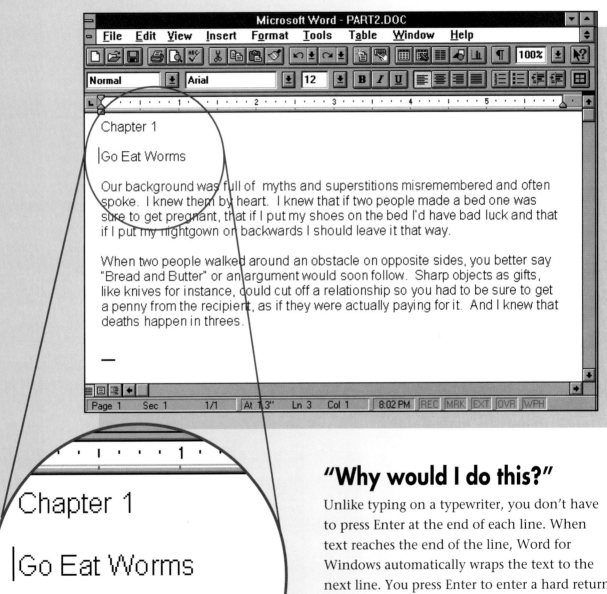

"Why would I do this?"

Unlike typing on a typewriter, you don't have to press Enter at the end of each line. When text reaches the end of the line, Word for Windows automatically wraps the text to the next line. You press Enter to enter a hard return at the end of a short line, to insert a blank line between paragraphs, or to end a paragraph.

Let's enter a hard return to end a paragraph. Then we will enter another hard return to insert a blank line.

Task 10: Inserting a Blank Line

1 Press **Ctrl+Home** to move to the top of the document. Click after *Chapter 1*. This step places the insertion point where you want to insert a blank line. Be sure to click after the 1.

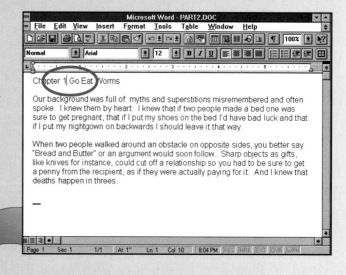

2 Press **Enter**. Pressing Enter ends the current paragraph, and Word for Windows inserts a paragraph mark in the document.

NOTE ▼

By default, paragraph marks (¶) do not appear on-screen. If you want to display paragraph marks, click the Show/Hide (¶) button on the Standard toolbar.

3 Press **Enter**. The first two lines are now separated by a blank line. Then, press **Delete** to delete the space. To delete a blank line, click at the beginning of the blank line and press the Delete key.

NOTE ▼

A hard return forces a line break. If you add or delete text, the hard return stays in the same position. A soft return is inserted by the program. When you add or delete text, the program adjusts the soft returns.

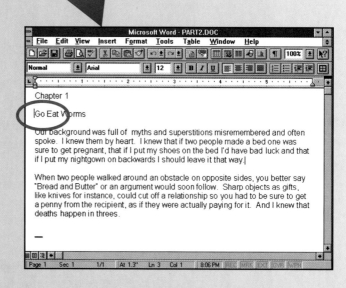

TASK 11
Combining Paragraphs

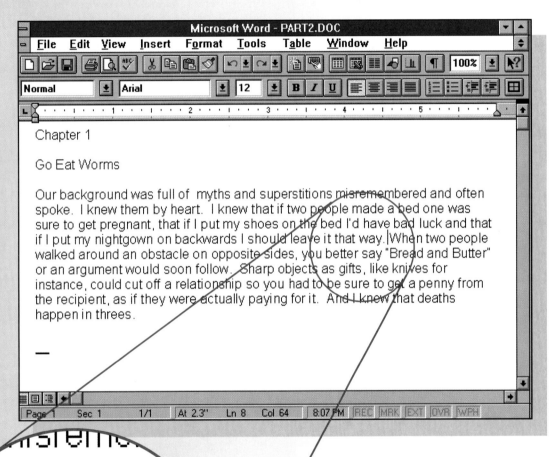

"Why would I do this?"

Sometimes, you might delete text within a paragraph and find that the remaining text in that paragraph should be combined with the text in the next paragraph. In Word for Windows, you can easily combine paragraphs by deleting the hard returns between paragraphs and inserting space between sentences.

Let's combine two paragraphs now.

Task 11: Combining Paragraphs

1 Click after *way.* at the end of the first paragraph. This step places the insertion point at the end of the first paragraph. Be sure to click after the period.

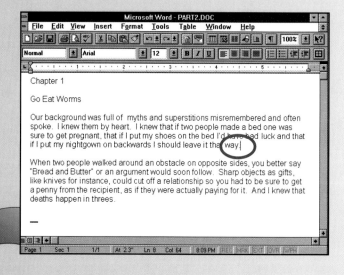

2 Press **Delete**. Pressing the Delete key deletes the paragraph mark at the end of the current paragraph.

NOTE ▼

By default, paragraph marks (¶) do not appear on-screen. If you want to display paragraph marks, click the Show/Hide (¶) button on the Standard toolbar.

3 Press **Delete** again. Then, press the **space bar**. Pressing the Delete key again deletes the blank line between the paragraphs. The second paragraph moves up next to the first paragraph. Pressing the space bar inserts a space between the two sentences.

WHY WORRY?

To split the paragraphs, place the insertion point where you want the break to appear. Then press Enter two times.

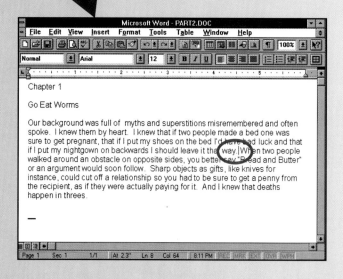

Inserting a Tab

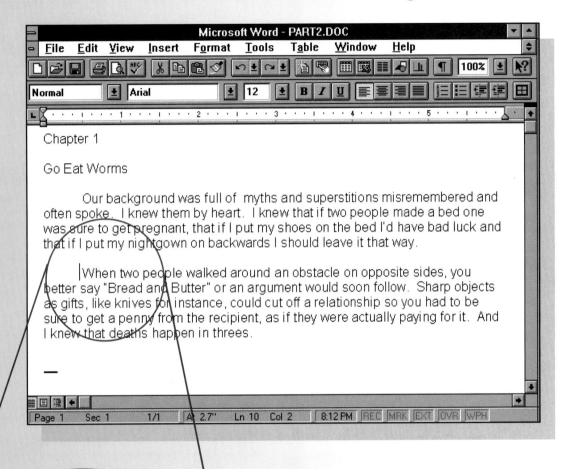

"Why would I do this?"

Just like typing on a typewriter, you press the Tab key to insert a tab. Perhaps you want to insert a tab at the beginning of a paragraph to indent the text from the left margin. You might want to use tabs in a memo heading to insert space between the headings and the memo information.

Let's insert a tab at the beginning of the paragraph.

Task 12: Inserting a Tab

1 Click before *Our* in the first sentence. The insertion point is where you want to insert a tab (at the beginning of the paragraph).

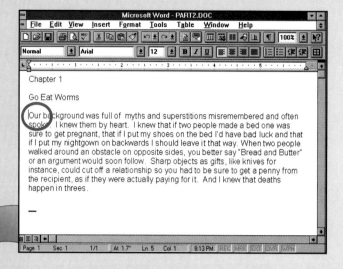

2 Press **Tab**. Pressing Tab inserts a tab and moves the insertion point to the next tab stop. As you can see, the first sentence begins at the tab stop. Word for Windows provides a default tab stop every 1/2 inch. You can also change the tab settings.

> **NOTE** ▼
>
> When you press the Tab key, Word for Windows inserts a tab mark in the document. By default, tab marks (→) do not appear on-screen. If you want to display tab marks, click the Show/Hide (¶) button on the Standard toolbar.

3 Click after *way*. Press **Enter** twice to end the first paragraph and insert a blank line. Then, press **Delete** to remove the space. Next, press **Tab** to insert a tab. As you can see, the first sentence in the paragraph begins at the tab stop.

> **WHY WORRY?**
>
> To delete the tab, press the Backspace key.

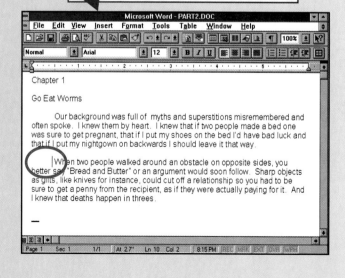

TASK 13

Inserting a
Page Break

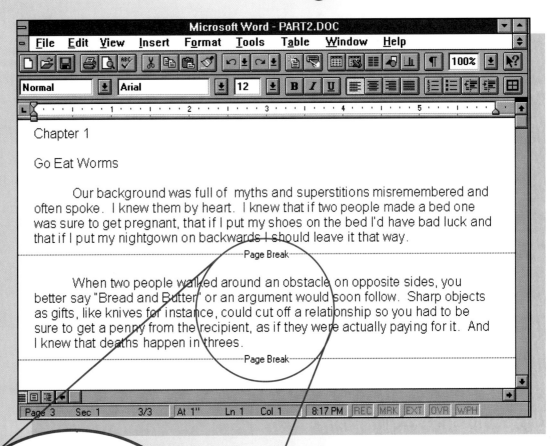

"Why would I do this?"

When the text reaches the end of a page, Word inserts a soft page break. The document repaginates, adjusting the locations of the soft page breaks. You can insert hard page breaks where you want one page to end and another to begin. Manual page breaks override automatic page breaks entered by Word.

Let's insert a page break at the end of the chapter. Then we will insert another page break below the second paragraph.

Task 13: Inserting a Page Break

1 Click before the tab (blank space) at the beginning of the second paragraph. This step places the insertion point where you want the new page to begin. Remember that you can place the insertion point by using the mouse or the arrow keys.

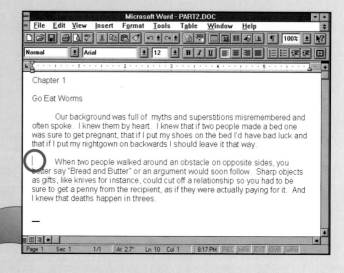

2 Press **Ctrl+Enter**. Pressing Ctrl+Enter inserts a hard page break in the document. A dotted line appears with the words Page Break in the middle. When you print the document, a new page will begin where you inserted the page break.

NOTE ▼

A soft page break appears as a dotted line on-screen. The dots are farther apart than those that indicate a hard page break.

3 Click at the beginning of the blank line below the second paragraph to place the insertion point where you want the new page to begin. Then, press **Ctrl+Enter** to insert a hard page break. The document now contains three pages.

WHY WORRY?

To remove the page break, click the Undo button on the Standard toolbar immediately after inserting the page break.

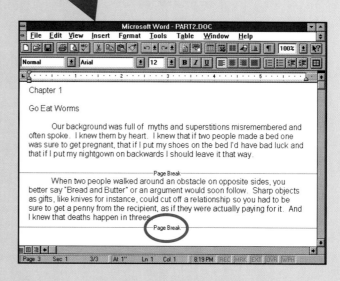

Going to a Specific Page

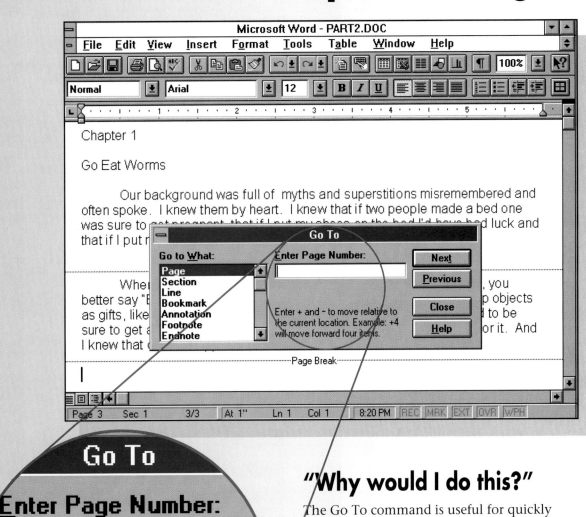

"Why would I do this?"

The Go To command is useful for quickly moving through pages in a document. You can jump to any page that is out of view in the current document. Perhaps you're working on page 4 and you want to make a change on page 1.

Let's move to page 1 using the Go To command.

Task 14: Going to a Specific Page

1 Click **Edit** then **Go To**. This selects the Go To command. Word for Windows opens the Go To dialog box. The insertion point is in the Enter Page Number text box.

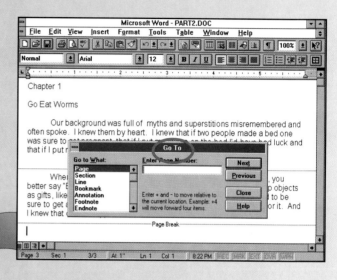

2 Type **1**. Typing 1 tells Word for Windows to go to page 1.

3 Press **Enter**. When you press Enter, page 1 becomes the current page. Click the **Close** button to close the Go To dialog box.

WHY WORRY?

If you mistakenly moved to the wrong page, repeat the Go To command, but type the correct page number to move to the page you want.

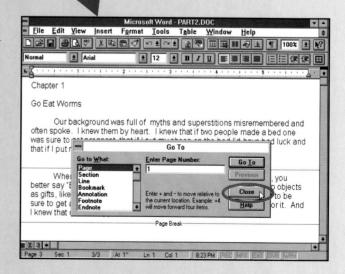

Selecting Text

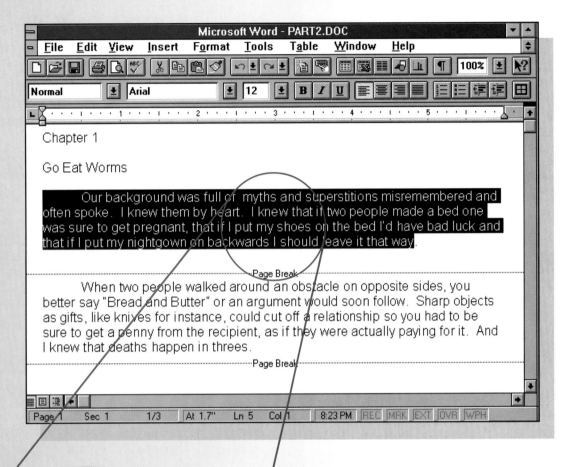

"Why would I do this?"

Knowing how to select text is essential because most of the commands and options in Word operate on the selected text. You can select any amount of text: a block of text, a word, a line, a sentence, and a paragraph with the mouse.

For example, there are times when you may want to perform a command on a line of text. Maybe you want to boldface a title or a heading.

First, let's select a section of text with the mouse. Next, we will select a word, then a line of text, a sentence, a paragraph, and a block of text.

Task 15: Selecting Text

1 Place the mouse pointer at the beginning of the text you want to select, hold down the left mouse button, and drag the mouse pointer across the text you want to select. This step selects the amount of text you specify.

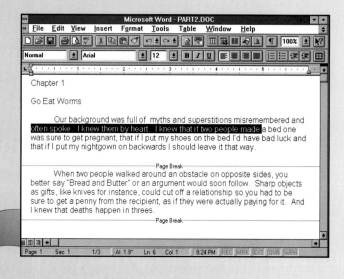

2 Double-click the word *superstitions*. This step selects only a word of text.

WHY WORRY?

Sometimes, you'll double-click a word to select and drag it, and do the third click (and hold) for the drag operation too quickly. Then the entire paragraph will be unintentionally selected. To avoid this, pause briefly and then perform your third click and hold.

3 Click the left margin next to the line of text. This step selects a line of text.

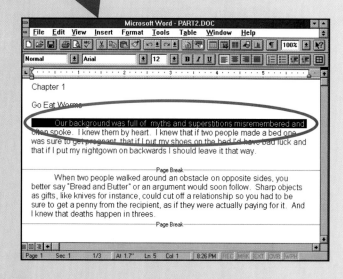

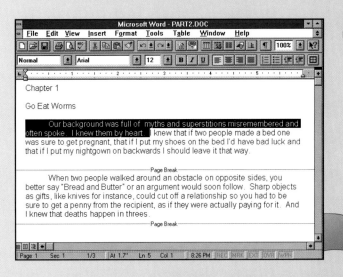

4 Hold down **Ctrl** and click anywhere within the sentence. This step selects a sentence.

5 Double-click the left margin next to the paragraph. This step selects a paragraph.

NOTE ▼

You can also triple-click the mouse anywhere inside the paragraph to select a paragraph.

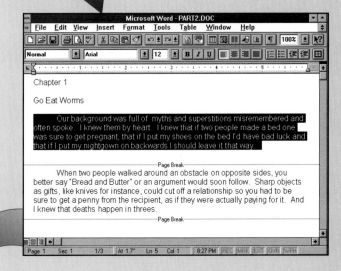

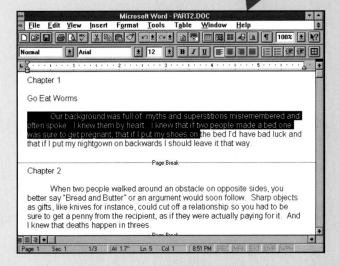

6 Position the mouse pointer at the beginning of the text you want to select, click the left mouse button, and then hold down **Shift** as you click the end of the block of text.

WHY WORRY?

If you selected the wrong text, simply click anywhere in the document. Then start over.

TASK 16
Deleting Text

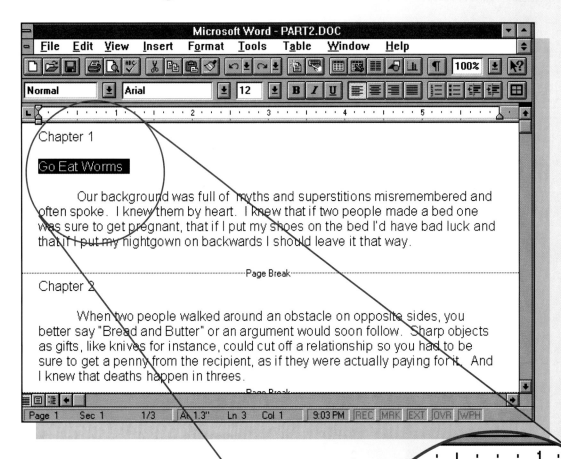

"Why would I do this?"

Sometimes you may find that text you initially typed into the document is incorrect and needs to be changed. Instead of overwriting the text to remove the entry, you can select any amount of text and then press the Delete key.

To delete just one character, use the Delete or Backspace key. The Delete key deletes the character to the right of the insertion point; the Backspace key deletes the character to the left of the insertion point.

In our document, let's assume the chapter title is incorrect. We will delete this line of text.

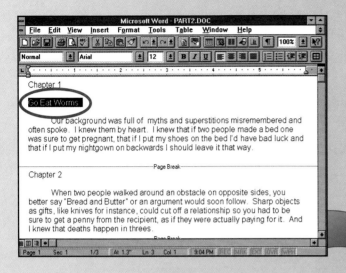

1 Click the left margin next to the chapter title. This step selects the words *Go Eat Worms*, the text you want to delete.

2 Press **Delete**. Word for Windows deletes the text. The remaining text moves up (or over) to fill in the gap.

WHY WORRY?

To restore the entry just deleted, click the Undo button on the Standard toolbar.

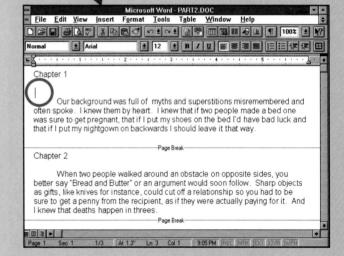

TASK 17

Copying Text

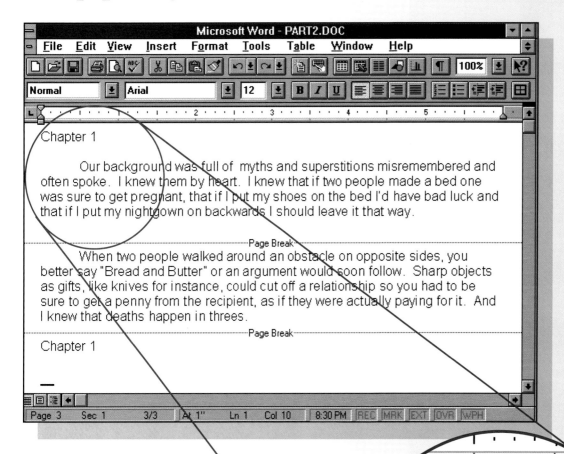

"Why would I do this?"

You can save the time of retyping information in the document by copying text over and over again. For example, you might want to copy a paragraph from one page to another page. That way, you wouldn't have to type the paragraph over again, saving you time and keystrokes.

Using the document, let's copy the chapter name Chapter 1 to the bottom of page 1. We can use the Copy and Paste buttons to quickly copy the line of text to the new location.

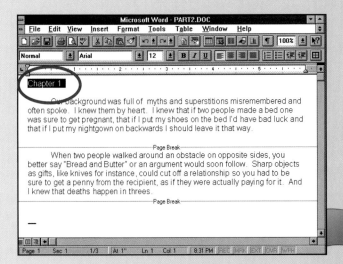

1 Click the left margin next to the chapter name. This step selects the text you want to copy—in this case, Chapter 1.

NOTE

To drag and drop text, select the text. Click and hold down the Ctrl key and the mouse button. You see a plus sign above and a small box under the mouse pointer. Drag the text to the new location. Release the Ctrl key and the mouse button.

2 Click the **Copy** button (the button that contains two pieces of paper) on the Standard toolbar. Clicking the Copy button copies the text to the Clipboard. The Clipboard is a temporary holding area for text and graphics.

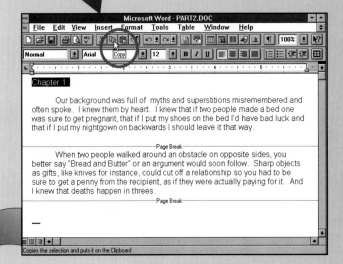

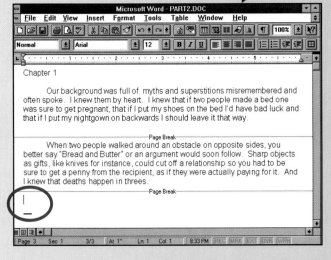

3 Click the blank line at the top of page 3. This step places the insertion point where you want the copied text to appear.

4 Click the **Paste** button (the button that contains a piece of paper on top of a clipboard) on the Standard toolbar. Clicking the Paste button selects the Paste command. The copied text now appears in the new location (as well as the original location).

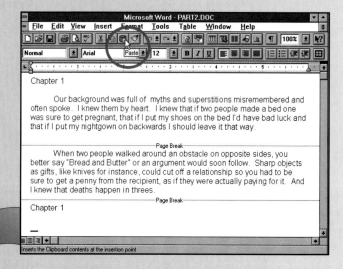

NOTE ▼

You can also use the Ctrl+C and Ctrl+V key combinations to select the Copy and Paste commands.

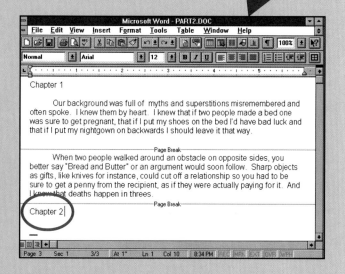

5 Click before the 1 in *Chapter 1*. Press **Insert**, type **2**, and press **Insert** again. This step changes the chapter number.

WHY WORRY?

If you copied the wrong text or copied the data to the wrong location, click the Undo button on the Standard toolbar to undo the most recent copy. Then start over. Or, just delete the copied text.

Moving Text

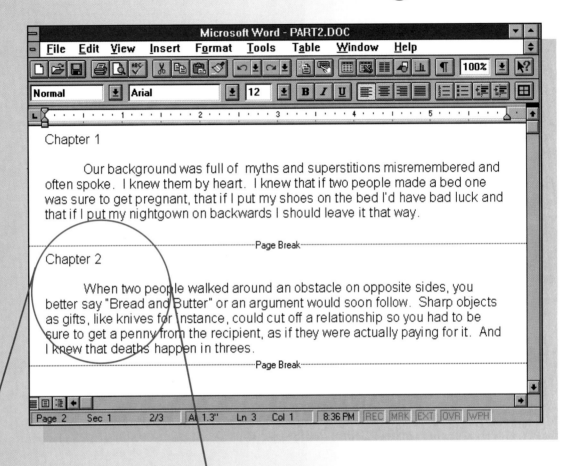

"Why would I do this?"

The Move command lets you move information from one location to another in the document. You don't have to go to the new location, enter the same text, and then erase the text in the old location.

For example, you might want to swap the order of paragraphs, or you might want to move text in a document because the layout of the document has changed. Suppose you want to move *Chapter 2* above the paragraph on page 2. Use the Cut and Paste buttons on the Standard toolbar to move the paragraph.

Task 18: Moving Text

1 Click the left margin next to *Chapter 2*. This step selects the text you want to move.

NOTE ▼

To drag and drop text, select the text. Click and hold down the mouse button. You see a small box under the mouse pointer. Drag the text to the new location. Release the mouse button.

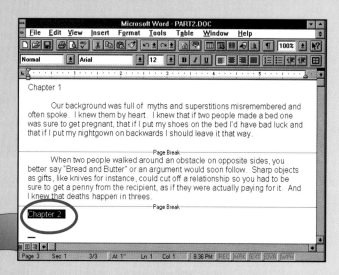

2 Click the **Cut** button (the button that contains a scissors) on the Standard toolbar. Clicking the Cut button cuts the text from the document and places it on the Clipboard (a temporary holding area).

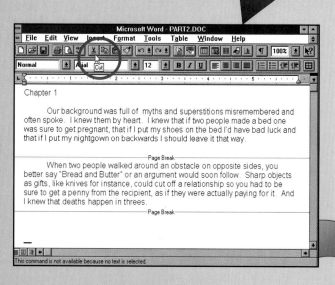

3 Click before the tab (the blank space) in the paragraph on page 2. This step places the insertion point where you want to move the text.

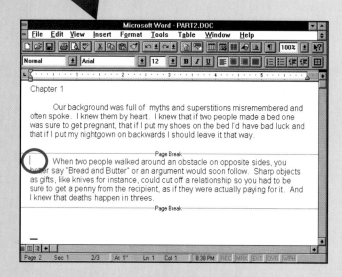

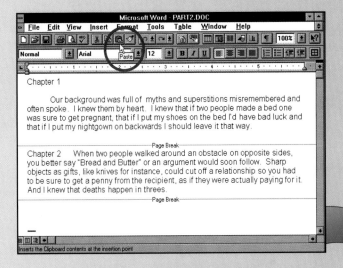

4 Click the **Paste** button (the button that contains a piece of paper on top of a clipboard) on the Standard toolbar to paste the text in the new location. The text now appears in the new location (but not in the original location).

NOTE ▼

You can also use the Ctrl+X and Ctrl+V key combinations to select the Cut and Paste commands.

5 Press **Enter** twice. This step inserts a hard return to end the short line and another hard page break to insert a blank line.

WHY WORRY?

If you moved the wrong text or moved the text to the wrong location, click the Undo button in the Standard toolbar to undo the most recent move. Then start over.

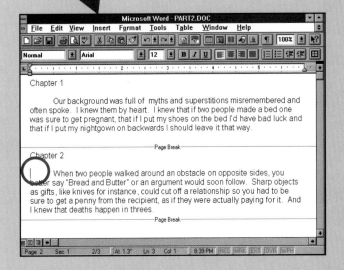

Using Undo

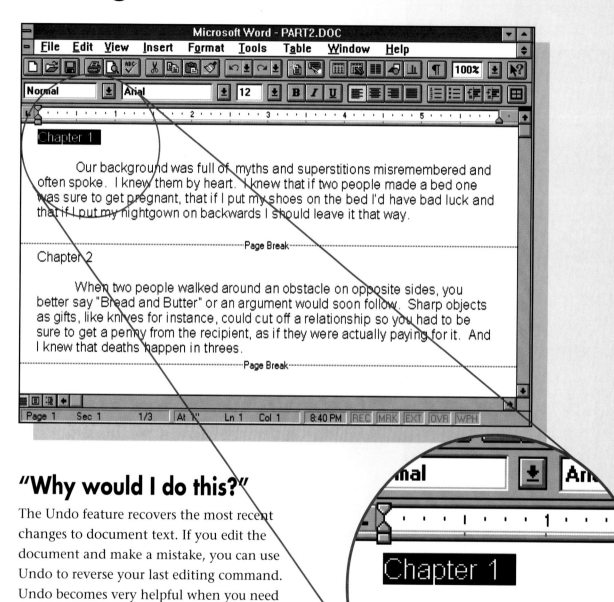

"Why would I do this?"

The Undo feature recovers the most recent changes to document text. If you edit the document and make a mistake, you can use Undo to reverse your last editing command. Undo becomes very helpful when you need to correct editing and formatting mistakes, especially when you delete text that you did not intend to delete.

Let's assume you no longer want the words Chapter 1 at the top of page 1, and you will delete the line of text. You can restore the deleted text by using the Undo feature.

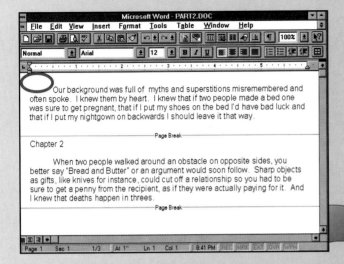

1 Press **Ctrl+Home** to move to the top of the document. Click the left margin next to Chapter 1 and press **Delete**. This step deletes the line of text. This is the deleted text you want to restore with Undo.

2 Click the **Undo** button (the button that contains an arrow that curves to the left and down) on the Standard toolbar. Clicking the Undo button selects the Undo command. Word for Windows restores the deleted text. As you can see, the document returns to its preceding form. Click outside the selected text to deselect the text.

WHY WORRY?

Click the Undo button a second time on the Standard toolbar to "undo" the Undo.

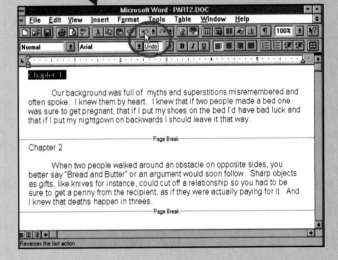

PART III

More Editing

20 Inserting the Date

21 Inserting a Special Character

22 Searching for Text

23 Replacing Text

24 Checking Your Spelling

25 Using the Thesaurus

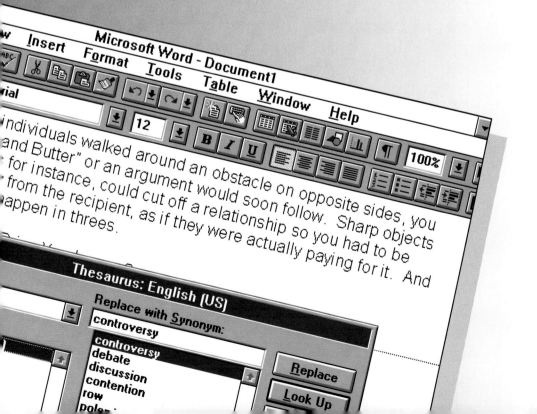

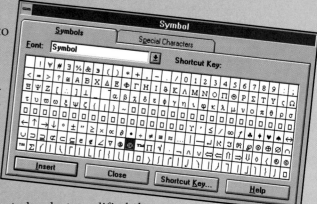

This part shows you how to insert the date, insert a special character, search for text, replace text, check your spelling, and use the thesaurus.

Word for Windows Date and Time feature enables you to enter dates and times in a document to show when you created or last modified the document. The following list shows the date and time formats available in Word.

8/22/94	8/22/94 1:04 PM
Sunday, August 22, 1994	8/22/94 1:04:10 PM
22 August, 1994	1:04 PM
August 22, 1994	1:04:10 PM
22-Aug-94	13:04
August, 94	13:04:10
Aug-94	

Special characters can include fonts such as Symbol and Wingdings, Greek letters, and scientific symbols. *Wingdings* are decorative characters such as bullets, stars, and flowers. You can choose the MS Line Draw font to insert foreign language characters such as tildes (~) and umlauts (¨).

Word for Windows provides bullets in various shapes and special characters such as em dashes (wide hyphens used in punctuation). There are two methods for entering special characters:

- You can use the Symbol dialog box, that shows a keyboard of special characters.

- You can use a series of special keystrokes that appear in a list when you choose the Special Characters tab in the Symbol dialog box.

The Find command enables you to search for specific text, character formats such as bold, italic, and underline, or paragraph formats such as indents and spacing. The text you search for can also include a special character, em and en dashes, manual page breaks, section breaks, carets, and any other special characters that appear in a document.

Word for Windows' Find and Replace feature lets you change a word or phrase, character formats, paragraph formats, or any special character throughout the document quickly and easily.

The search text can have a maximum of 255 characters. The Find command and the Replace command give you several search options to hone the search. The Search option specifies the direction of the search in the document. You can choose All to search the entire document from the insertion point, Down to search forward, and Up to search backward in the document. The Match Case option searches for text with the specified combination of upper- and lowercase letters.

The Find Whole Words Only (a space before a group of letters and a space after) search option searches for whole words only and does not find occurrences of the word that are part of other words. The Use Pattern Matching option searches for patterns in formatting, such as indented paragraphs and numbered headings. The Sounds Like option searches for homonyms, which are words that sound like the current word for which you are searching.

With the Spelling feature, you can use custom dictionaries for medical, legal, and technical documents to ensure accuracy when spell-checking special terms for documents in those fields.

The Thesaurus feature is very useful for looking up synonyms and antonyms for words used in your document.

This part will introduce you to some of Word for Windows' time-saving features for editing text in your documents.

controversy

debate

discussion

contention

quarrel

altercation

feud

Inserting the Date

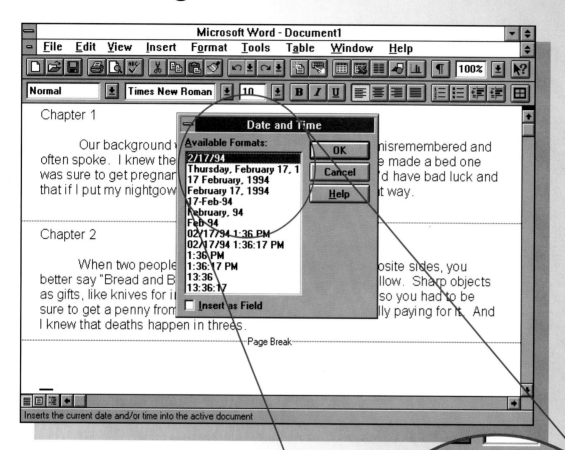

"Why would I do this?"

The Date and Time command inserts the date or time into a document automatically. The date and time are received from the computer's clock. Word for Windows inserts the current date and time when you open the document. You might want to insert the date into a letter or memo automatically instead of typing the date. Dates in a document can also help you keep track of the last time you modified your document.

In our document, let's insert the date now.

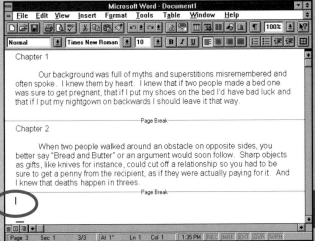

1 Click at the top of page 3. This step places the insertion point where you want the date to appear.

NOTE ▼

Because Word for Windows uses the computer's clock to insert the current date and time, you must ensure that the computer's clock is set to the correct date and time.

2 Click **Insert** on the menu bar. This step opens the Insert menu. You see a list of Insert commands.

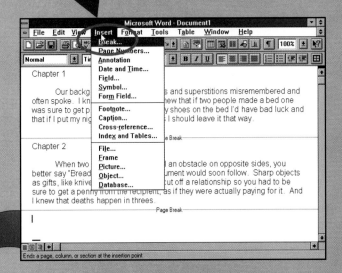

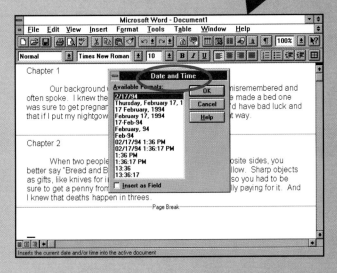

3 Click **Date and Time**. This step selects the Date and Time command. You see the Date and Time dialog box. This dialog box lists the available date and time formats.

Task 20: Inserting the Date

4 Click the fourth format from the top. This step selects the date format. You see the current date in the dialog box.

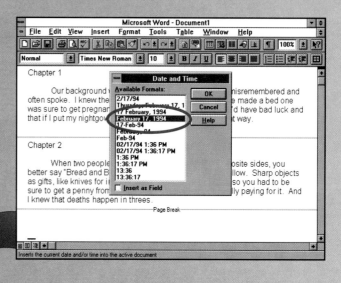

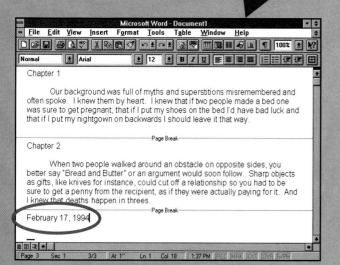

5 Click **OK**. This step confirms the command. Word for Windows inserts a special code (called a *field code*) in the document, and you see the current date on-screen. For information on field codes (how to display and use them), see your Microsoft Word for Windows documentation.

NOTE ▼

When you insert the date, Word for Windows inserts a field code (which you do not see in Normal view). If you try to backspace to delete the date, you hear a beep. To delete the date, you must select the entire date and then press the Delete key.

WHY WORRY?

To delete the date, click the Undo button in the Standard toolbar immediately after you insert the date.

Inserting a Special Character

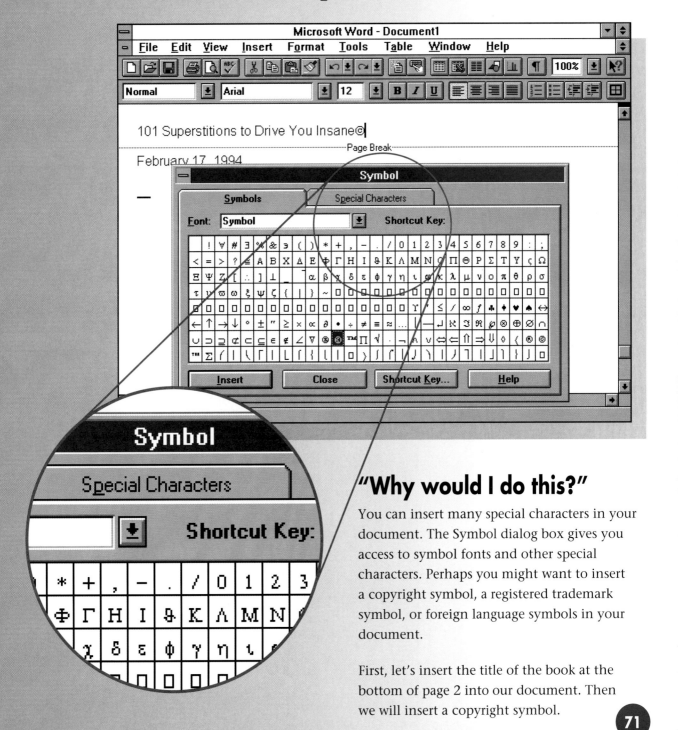

"Why would I do this?"

You can insert many special characters in your document. The Symbol dialog box gives you access to symbol fonts and other special characters. Perhaps you might want to insert a copyright symbol, a registered trademark symbol, or foreign language symbols in your document.

First, let's insert the title of the book at the bottom of page 2 into our document. Then we will insert a copyright symbol.

Task 21: Inserting a Special Character

1 Click after *threes.* at the end of the paragraph on page 2. Then, press Enter twice. Next, type **101 Superstitions to Drive You Insane**. This step enters the title of the book.

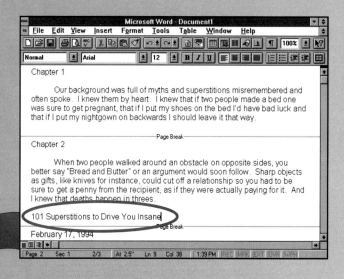

2 Click **Insert** on the menu bar. This step opens the Insert menu. You see a list of Insert commands.

3 Click **Symbol**. This step selects the Symbol command. You see the Symbol dialog box. This dialog box has two tabs, one for symbols and one for special characters. By default, the Symbols tab is displayed.

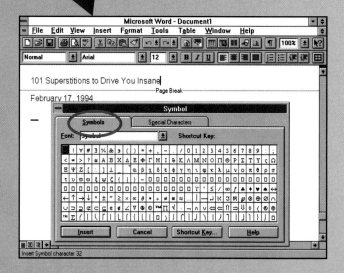

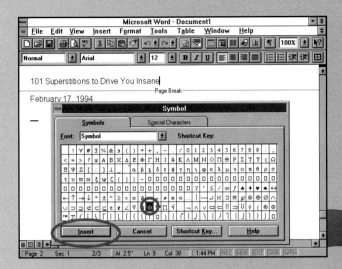

4 Click the copyright symbol (©). This step selects the symbol you want to insert. Click the **Insert** button.

5 Word for Windows inserts the symbol. Then, click **Close**. This step closes the dialog box. The selected symbol will now be placed in the document at the insertion point.

WHY WORRY?

To undo the insertion, click the Undo icon in the toolbar or delete by pressing Backspace or Delete.

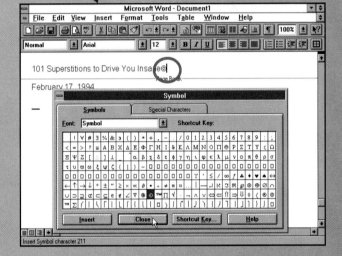

Searching for Text

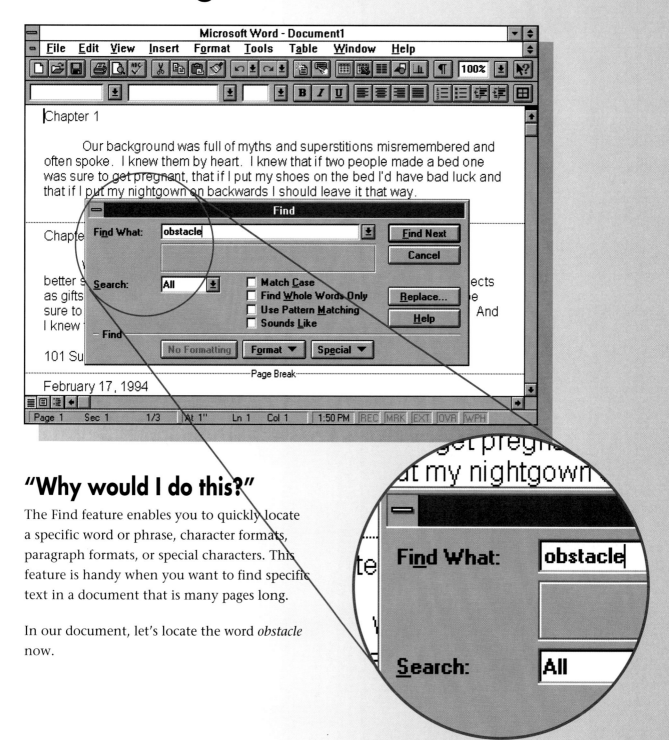

"Why would I do this?"

The Find feature enables you to quickly locate a specific word or phrase, character formats, paragraph formats, or special characters. This feature is handy when you want to find specific text in a document that is many pages long.

In our document, let's locate the word *obstacle* now.

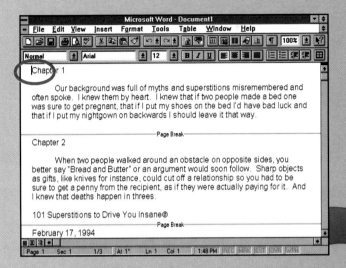

1 Press **Ctrl+Home**. This step moves the insertion point to the beginning of the document. When you begin the search, Word for Windows searches from the location of the insertion point forward.

NOTE ▼

If you start searching when the insertion point is in the middle of the document, Word for Windows searches from that location to the end of the document and then displays a message box that asks whether you want to continue searching from the beginning.

2 Press **Ctrl+F**. Pressing Ctrl+F selects the Edit Find command. You see the Find dialog box. The insertion point is in the Find What text box.

NOTE ▼

The Find dialog box includes the Find What text box and other options that control how the program searches the document.

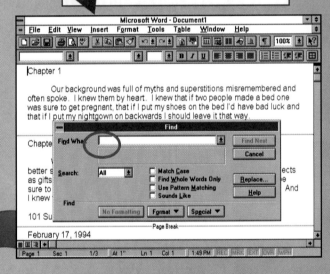

3 Type **obstacle**. This text, called the *search string*, is what you want to find.

NOTE ▼

By default, Word finds any occurrence of this text, regardless of the case. You can specify that you want to find only whole words and to match case. To do so, click the Match Case or Find Whole Words Only check boxes.

Task 22: Searching for Text

4 Click **Find Next**. This step selects the Find Next button and starts the search. Word for Windows finds the first occurrence of the search string and selects that text. The dialog box remains open on-screen.

NOTE ▼
To search for the next occurrence of the search string, click the Find Next button again.

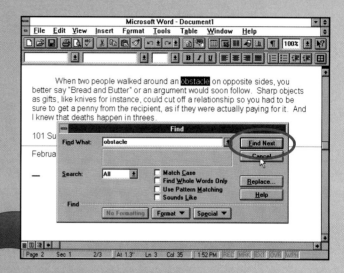

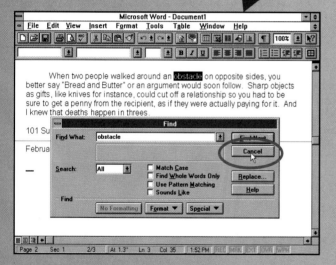

5 Click **Cancel**. This step chooses the Cancel button and closes the dialog box.

NOTE ▼
You can also close the dialog box and press Shift+F4 to repeat the search.

WHY WORRY?
If Word for Windows does not find the text, you see an alert message. Click OK and try the search again. Be sure to type the search string correctly.

TASK 23
Replacing Text

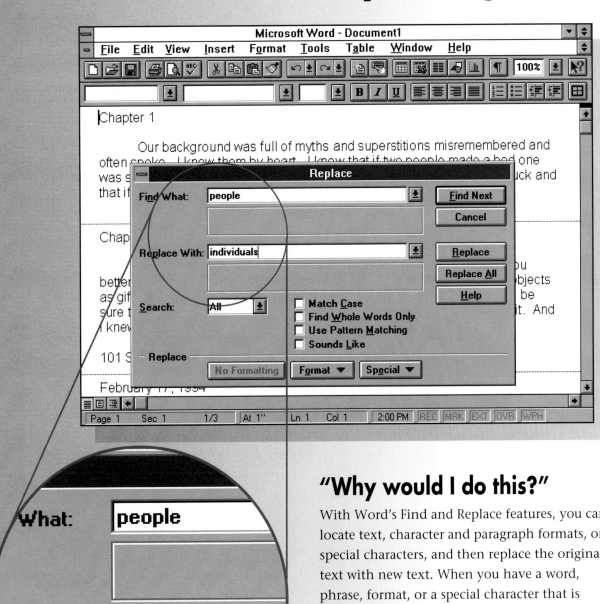

"Why would I do this?"

With Word's Find and Replace features, you can locate text, character and paragraph formats, or special characters, and then replace the original text with new text. When you have a word, phrase, format, or a special character that is entered incorrectly throughout the document, you can use the Edit Replace command to search and replace all occurrences of the incorrect information with the correct information. In our document, let's assume that the word *people* is incorrect. The word *people* should be *individuals*. Let's replace all occurrences of *people* with *individuals*.

Task 23: Replacing Text

1 Press **Ctrl+Home**. This step moves the insertion point to the beginning of the document. When you begin the search, Word for Windows searches from the location of the insertion point forward.

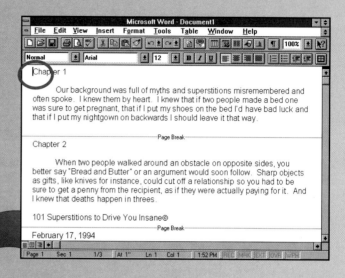

NOTE ▼

If you start searching when the insertion point is in the middle of the document, Word for Windows searches from that location to the end of the document and then displays a message box that asks whether you want to continue searching from the beginning.

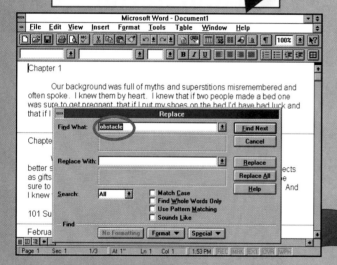

2 Press **Ctrl+H**. Pressing Ctrl+H selects the Edit Replace command. Word displays the Replace dialog box. The insertion point is in the Find What text box. Notice the previous search string appears in the Find What box.

NOTE ▼

The Replace dialog box includes the Find What text box, the Replace With text box, and other options that control how the program performs the search and replace operation.

3 Type **people** and press **Tab**. This text, called the *search string*, is what you want to find. Pressing Tab moves the insertion point to the Replace With text box.

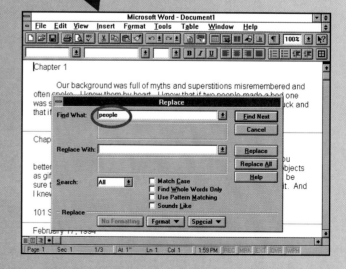

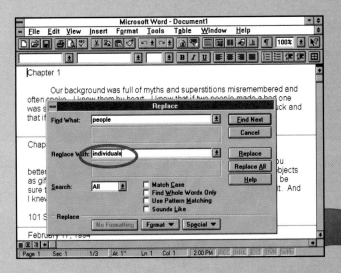

4 Type **individuals**. This is the text you want to use as the replacement.

5 Click **Find Next.** This step selects the Find Next button and starts the search. Word for Windows finds the first occurrence of the search string and selects that text. The dialog box remains open on-screen. (You can move the dialog box to see other text by dragging the dialog box's title bar.)

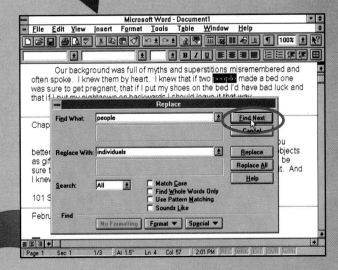

6 Click **Replace.** This step replaces the selected text with the next text and then moves to the next occurrence of the search string. The dialog box remains open on-screen.

Task 23: Replacing Text

7 Click **Replace.** This step selects the Replace button again. Word replaces the selected occurrence of the text and then moves to the next occurrence of the search string. When Word finds no more occurrences of the search string, you see an alert box.

NOTE ▼

To replace all occurrences of the text automatically, click the Replace All button. Be careful; make test replacements before you choose Replace All.

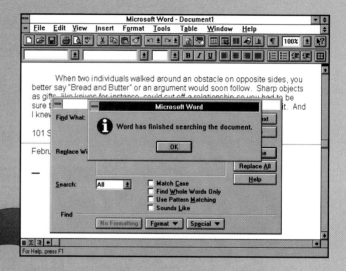

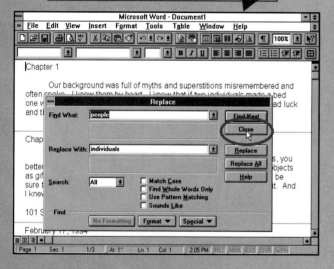

8 Click **OK.** This step closes the alert box. The dialog box remains open. Click **Close** to close the dialog box. Now you can see the replaced text.

WHY WORRY?

If Word for Windows does not find the text, you see an alert message. Click OK and try the search again. Be sure to type the search string correctly.

Checking Your Spelling

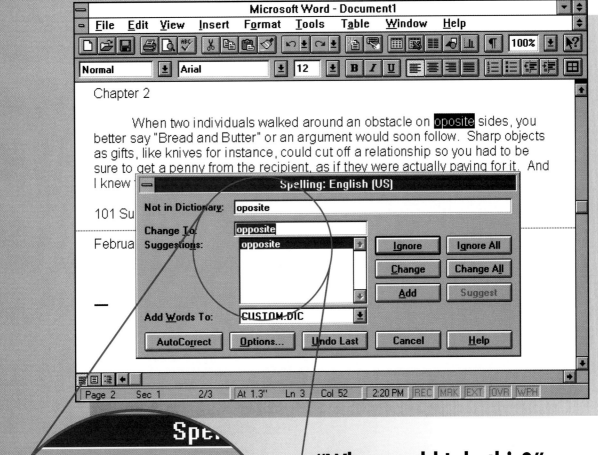

"Why would I do this?"

Word's spell checker finds and highlights for correction the misspellings in a document. Spell-checking is an important feature that makes your documents look professional and letter perfect. If there are any misspelled words in your document, Word will find them. However, just to make sure that Word finds some spelling errors, make an intentional typo. First make a spelling error in the word *opposite*. Then, run the spell checker and correct the misspelled words.

Task 24: Checking Your Spelling

1 On page 2 in the document, in the first sentence, remove the first occurrence of the letter p in the word *opposite*.

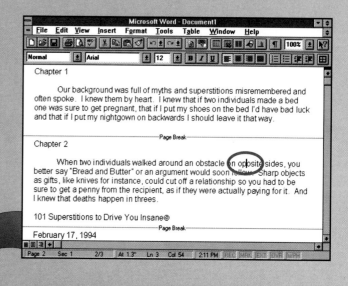

2 Press **Ctrl+Home**. This step moves the insertion point to the document's beginning. When you begin the spell check, Word checks from the insertion point forward.

NOTE ▼

If you start the spell check when the insertion point is in the middle of the document, Word checks from that location to the end of the document and then displays a message box that asks whether you want to continue checking spelling from the beginning of the document.

3 Click the **Spelling** button on the toolbar to find the first misspelled word and display the Spelling dialog box. The word appears in the Not in Dictionary text box. A suggested spelling appears in the Change To text box with more suggestions beneath it.

NOTE ▼

The Spelling dialog box lists suggested spellings for the word not found in the dictionary. You can select from several spelling options to correct the error.

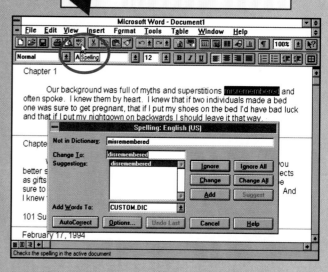

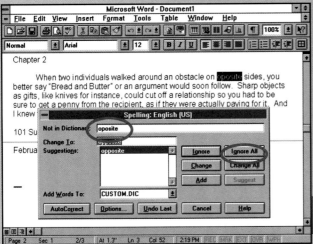

4 Click **Ignore All**. This option tells Word for Windows to ignore all occurrences of this word (that is, not to stop on this word again). The spell checker finds the next misspelled word oposite and displays the word at the top of the Spelling dialog box.

NOTE ▼

The Spelling dialog box covers up the change in the document, but you will be able to see the change when Spelling is complete and the dialog box is removed from the screen.

5 Click **Change**. This step replaces the incorrect word with the correct word in the document. The spell checker doesn't find any more misspelled words and displays the prompt: The spell checking is complete.

WHY WORRY?

To stop the spell check, click Cancel after Word for Windows stops on a word.

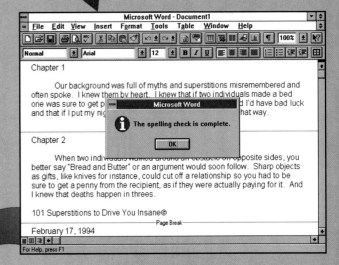

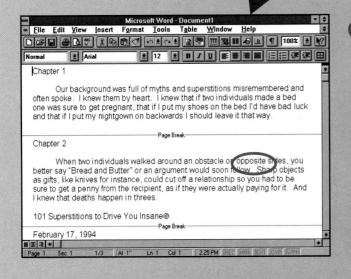

6 Click **OK**. This confirms that spell checking is complete. Now you can see the corrected spelling error in the word opposite in the first sentence on page 2.

WHY WORRY?

If you mistakenly select the wrong Spell option, you can click the Undo Last button in the Spelling dialog box to undo the last option you chose, or you can correct the mistake after you exit the spell checker.

Using the Thesaurus

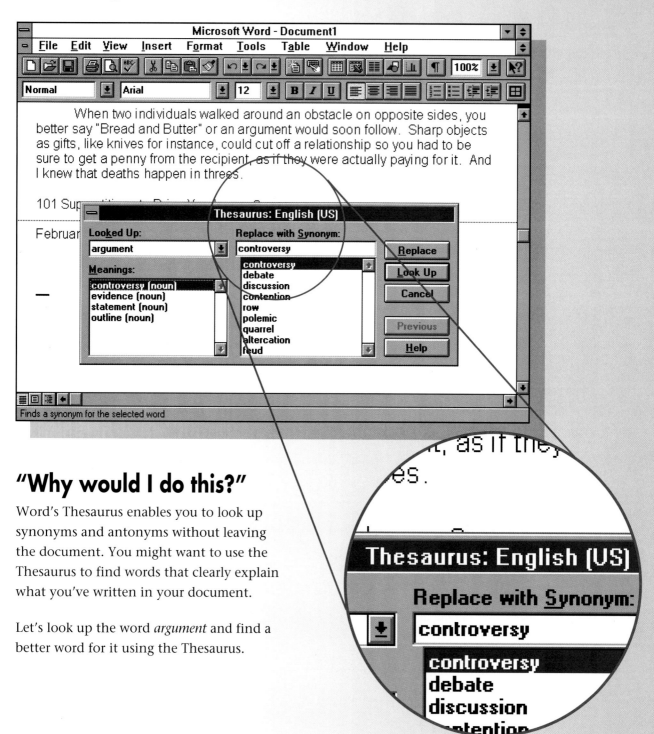

"Why would I do this?"

Word's Thesaurus enables you to look up synonyms and antonyms without leaving the document. You might want to use the Thesaurus to find words that clearly explain what you've written in your document.

Let's look up the word *argument* and find a better word for it using the Thesaurus.

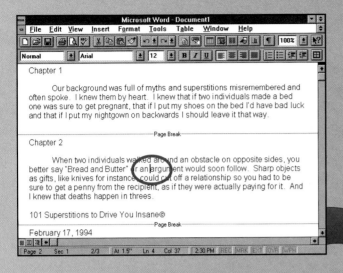

1 Click before the word *argument*. You can click before the word or within the word you want to look up.

2 Press **Shift+F7** to select the Thesaurus command. You see the Thesaurus dialog box. The Looked Up text box displays the selected word; beneath this box you see a list of meanings. To the right of the Looked Up box, you see a list of synonyms; the first synonym is selected and appears in the Replace with Synonym.

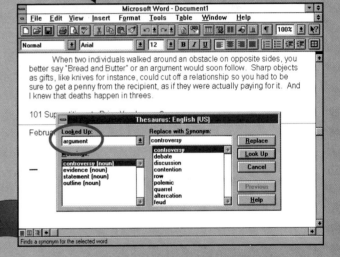

NOTE ▼

The Thesaurus feature offers many options. You can display additional synonyms or antonyms to clarify your document.

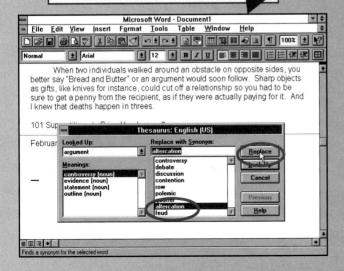

3 Click **altercation**. This step selects the word *altercation* in the Replace with Synonym list box. Then, click **Replace** to select the Replace button. Word replaces *argument* with *altercation*, and closes the dialog box.

WHY WORRY?

To undo the replacement, click the Undo button in the Standard toolbar immediately.

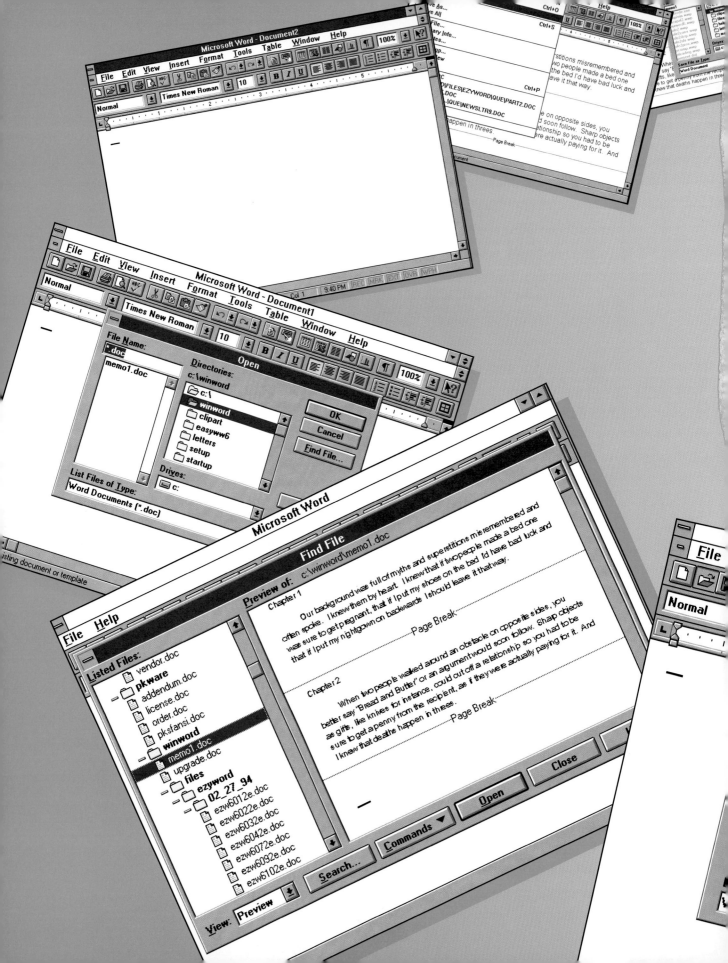

PART IV

Managing Files

26 Saving a Document

27 Closing a Document

28 Creating a New Document

29 Opening a Document

30 Finding a Document

This part gives you details about managing document files in Word. You learn how to save your work, abandon a document, create a new document, open a document, find a document, and close a document.

By default, Word automatically saves your work every 10 minutes. You can change the time interval or you can turn off the automatic save feature altogether. To make changes to the automatic save feature, from the Tools menu, choose Options; then click the Save tab. Type the number of minutes in the Automatic Save text box. To turn off automatic save, click the Automatic Save's check box again to remove the X and then click OK.

It is a good idea to save your file every 5 or 10 minutes. If you don't save your work, you could lose it. Suppose that you have been working on a document for a few hours and your power goes off unexpectedly—an air conditioning repairman at your office shorts out the power, a thunderstorm hits, or something else causes a power loss. If you haven't saved, you lose all your hard work. Of course, you should also make backup copies on floppy disks from time to time.

Saving a file that you previously saved is slightly different from saving a newly created document. When you save a document you saved before, you save the current version on-screen and overwrite the original version on disk. This means you always have the most current version of your file stored on disk.

If you want to keep both versions—the on-screen version and the original—you can use the File Save As command to save the on-screen version with a different name. Saving a file with a new name gives you two copies of the same document with differences in their data. When you save a file with a new name, you also can save the file in a different directory or drive.

Saving a document does not remove it from the screen. This requires closing the document. Whether you've saved a document or not, you can close it using the File Close command.

You can open more than one document at a time. For example, you might have two separate documents that contain related information. While using one document, you can view the information in another. Having both documents open and in view makes this possible. The number of documents you can open simultaneously depends on the amount of working memory available in your computer.

When you open several documents, they overlap and hide documents beneath other documents. Word lets you rearrange the documents so that some part of each document is visible. Arranging the open windows into smaller windows of similar sizes is handy when you want to copy or move text between two documents side by side. You can use the Arrange All command to arrange the windows into smaller windows. If you want to display a single document after you are finished using the window arrangement. Click the document window to make it active. Then click the maximize button in the top right corner. The document you want to display fills the screen.

Word's Find File command lets you search for a document using any search criteria. For example, you can find a document on a disk by its file name or directory as search criteria. You can choose the Find File command on the File menu or when you choose the Open command, you can click the Find File button in the Open dialog box. Either way, Word can quickly find the file you want to use.

In this part, you are introduced to the essential file management skills that you will need in order to work with any files in Word.

TASK 26
Saving a Document

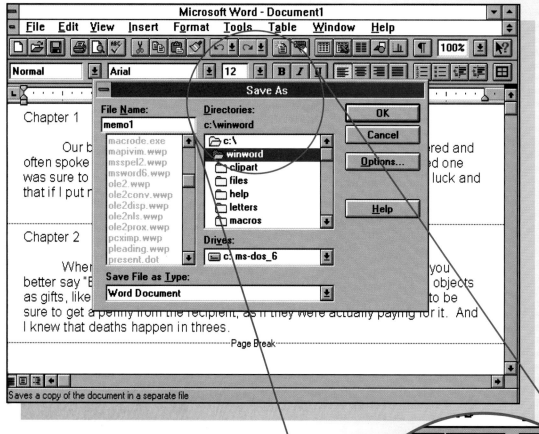

"Why would I do this?"

Until you save the document, your data is not stored on disk. You can lose your data if something, such as a power loss, happens. When you need the document again, you can retrieve it from the disk. Save your work every few minutes and at the end of a work session. Then close the document to clear the screen. Word also lets you close a previously saved document without saving changes.

Now save the document you have been working on in the previous tasks. Name the file MEMO1.

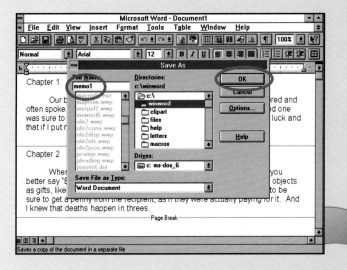

1 Click the **Save** button on the Standard toolbar. The first time you save the document, Word displays the **Save As** dialog box. The Save As dialog box lists current directories and the current drive. Type **memo1** in the File Name text box. This is the file name you want to assign to the document. You can type as many as eight characters.

2 Click **OK**. This step accepts the file name and returns you to the document. The file name, MEMO1.DOC, appears in the title bar.

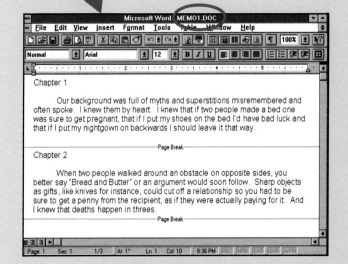

NOTE ▼

Use only alphanumeric characters in the file name when saving files; don't use spaces or punctuation marks. You can type either upper- or lowercase characters. You do not have to retype an extension. Word automatically adds the .DOC extension.

WHY WORRY?

If you type a file name that already exists, Word displays an alert box that asks `Replace existing file?` Click Cancel to return to the Save As dialog box, and then type a new name.

Closing a Document

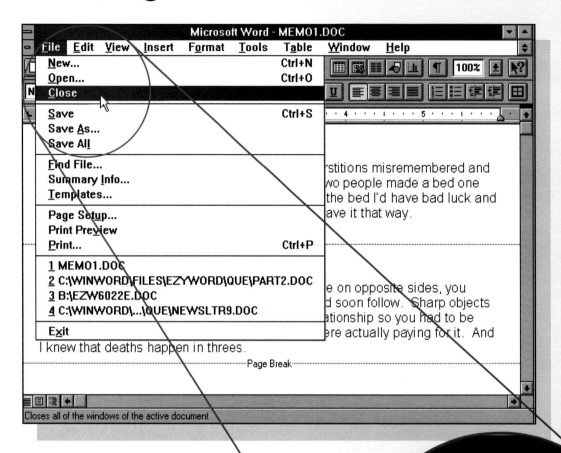

"Why would I do this?"

When you no longer want to work with a document, you can use the File Close command to close the document. You then can use the Open button on the Standard toolbar to reopen a closed document, or use the New button on the Standard toolbar to create a new document or exit Word.

Close the MEMO1.DOC document file.

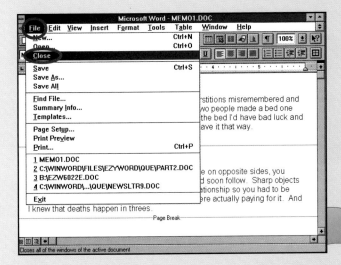

1 Click **File** in the menu bar. This step opens the File menu.

2 Click **Close**. This step selects the File Close command. Word closes the document. You see just two menu options: File and Help. From here, you can open a document or create a new document.

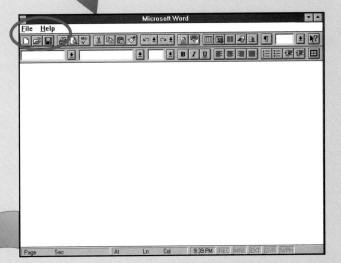

NOTE ▼

You can also use the Control menu box in the upper left corner of the document window on the left end of the menu bar to close the file—simply double-click the Control menu box.

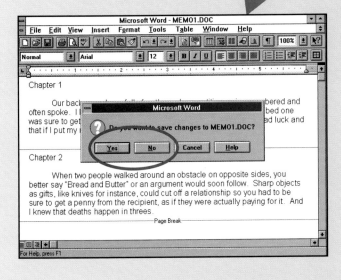

3 If you have made changes, Word displays an alert box that reminds you to save the changes. Choose Yes to save the changes and close the document. If you don't want to save the changes, choose No to ignore them and close the document.

WHY WORRY?

If you decide that you do need to make changes, click Cancel in the alert box. Word takes you back to the document.

TASK 28
Creating a New Document

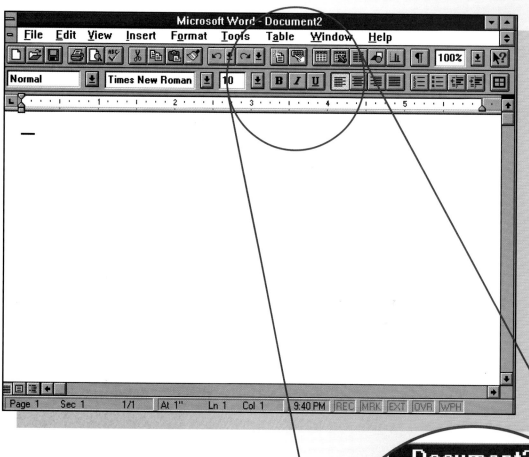

"Why would I do this?"

Word presents a new, blank document when you first start the program. You can create another new document at any time. Perhaps you have saved and closed the active document and want to begin a new one.

Create a new document and see how it works. Then you abandon the new document.

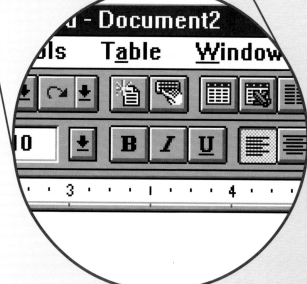

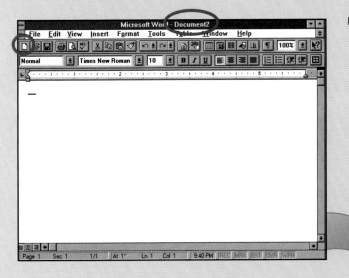

1 Click the **New** button in the Standard toolbar. Clicking the New button selects the **File New** command. A blank document appears on-screen. This document is titled DOCUMENT2 (the number varies depending on the number of documents you have created during this session).

NOTE ▼

When you start Word, the program automatically displays a blank document. You don't have to use the File New command in this case.

2 Click **File** in the menu bar and then click **Close**. This step selects the File Close command. Word closes the document. As you can see, there are two menu options: File and Help. In the next task, you open a document.

WHY WORRY?

If you don't want to create a new document, abandon the document.

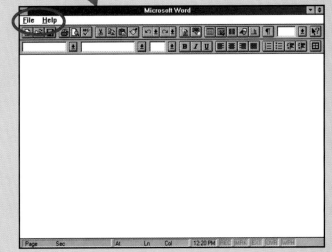

TASK 29
Opening a Document

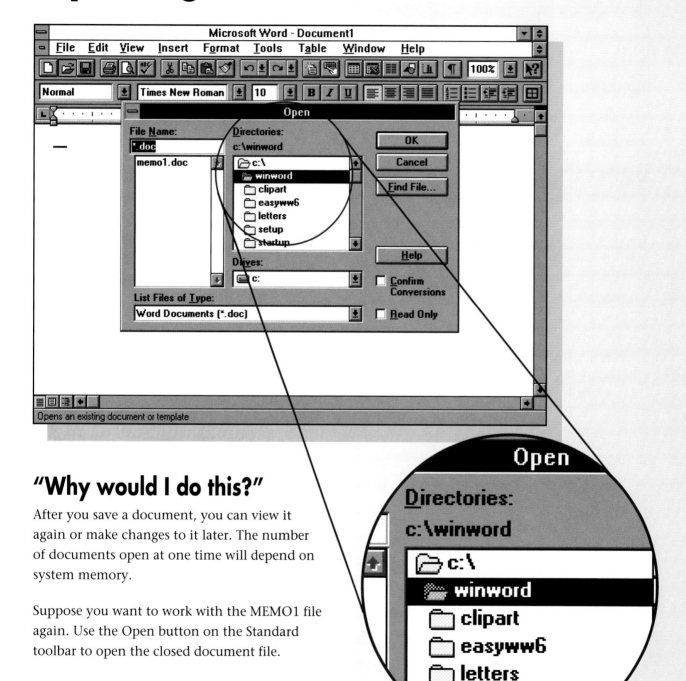

"Why would I do this?"

After you save a document, you can view it again or make changes to it later. The number of documents open at one time will depend on system memory.

Suppose you want to work with the MEMO1 file again. Use the Open button on the Standard toolbar to open the closed document file.

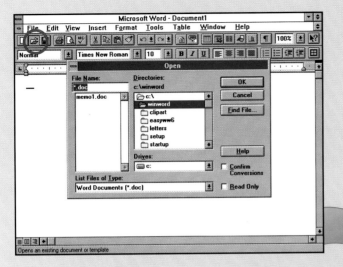

1 Click the **Open** button in the Standard toolbar. Clicking the Open button selects the File Open command. You see the Open dialog box. The insertion point is in the File Name text box.

NOTE ▼

The Open dialog box also contains the Files list and the Directories list. If the file is stored in a different directory, double-click the directory name in the Directories list. To move up a directory level, double-click [. .].

2 If necessary, click the down scroll arrow in the File Name list to find the MEMO1.DOC file. MEMO1.DOC is the name of the file you want to open. When you see the file, double-click it. This step selects the file and opens the document. Word displays the document on-screen. The file name appears in the title bar.

NOTE ▼

You can type the file name if you know it, or you can use the mouse to select the file name in the File Name list.

WHY WORRY?

If you open the wrong document, close the document and try again.

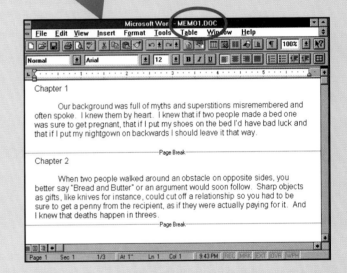

Finding a Document

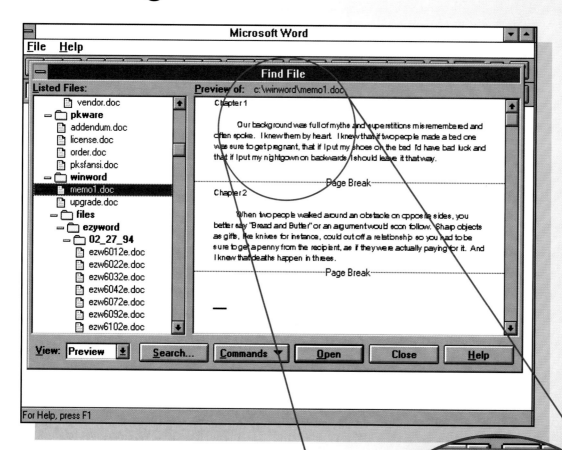

"Why would I do this?"

Word's Find File feature enables you to search for a single file or group of files based on search criteria you specify. When Word finds the files, you can perform a variety of operations on them such as preview, print, delete, copy, sort, and much more. The Find File command is handy when you can't remember the name of a file.

Find the MEMO1.DOC with the Find File command.

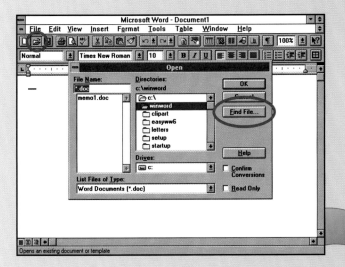

1 Click the **Open** button on the Standard toolbar. This step selects the File Open command. Word displays the Open dialog box.

> **NOTE** ▼
>
> You can enter search criteria in the Saved Searches text box and specify advanced search criteria. For information on other dialog box options, see your Microsoft Word documentation.

2 Click the **Find File** button in the Open dialog box. This step opens the Search dialog box. The insertion point appears in the File Name text box. Note *.doc is the current file name and file type. This means that Word searches for all Microsoft Word document files.

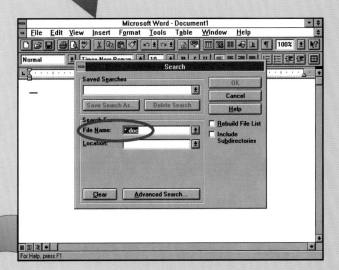

3 Click the down arrow button next to the **Location** text box to see a list of drives. Next, click **c:**. Then click in the check box next to **Include Subdirectories**. This step tells Word which drive you want to search and that you want to search for Microsoft Word files in all subdirectories.

4 Click **OK**. This step confirms your choices. Word displays the Find File window. A list of subdirectories and files appears on the left side of the window. In the third subdirectory from the top of the list, WINWORD, the MEMO1.DOC file, in this case, appears in the list.

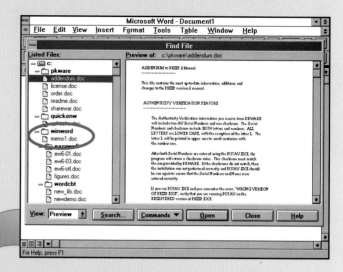

5 Click MEMO1.DOC in the list. The MEMO1.DOC document appears in the Preview window on the right.

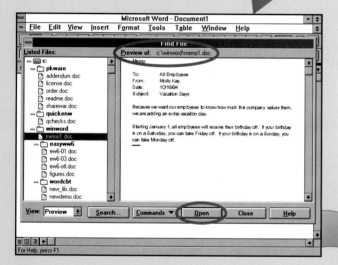

> **NOTE** ▼
>
> The View options and the Search, Commands, and Open buttons appear at the bottom of the dialog box. For information on other dialog box options, refer to your Microsoft Word documentation.

6 Click the **Open** button in the Find File window. This step opens the selected file. Word displays the document on-screen with the file name in the title bar.

> **WHY WORRY?**
>
> Word displays the `No matching files found` message when the program doesn't find any files based on the specified search criteria. Just click the Search button in the Find File window and try again.

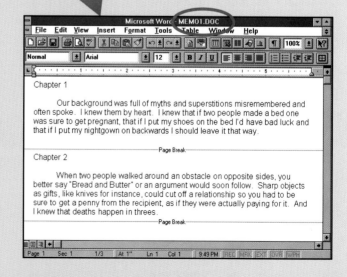

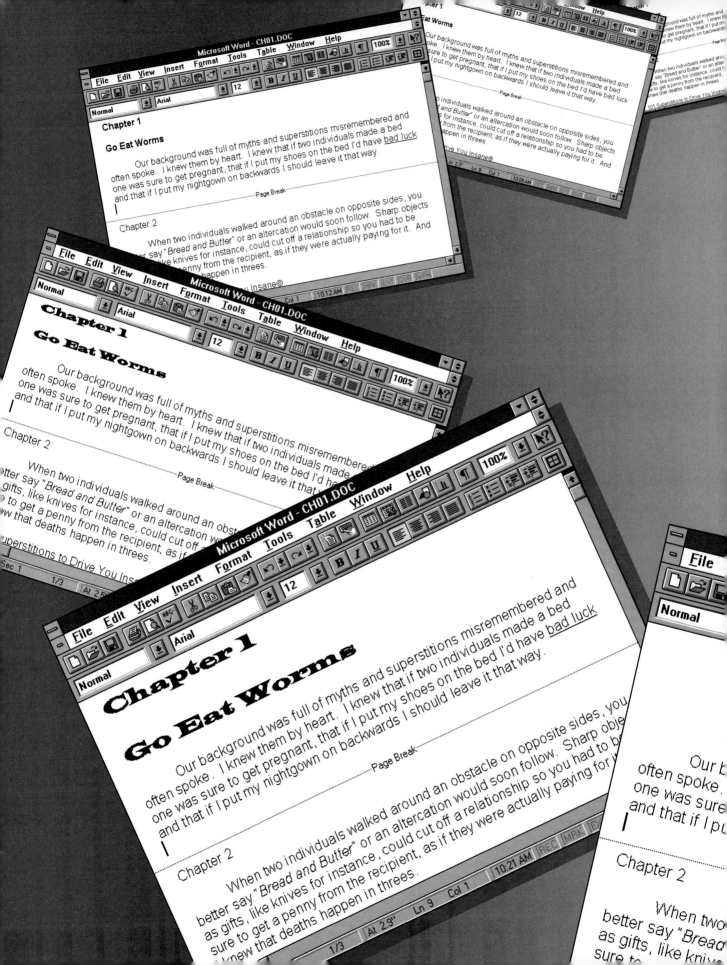

PART V

Formatting

31 Making Text Bold

32 Italicizing Text

33 Underlining Text

34 Changing the Font

35 Changing the Font Size

36 Centering Text

37 Aligning Text Flush Right

38 Indenting Text

39 Creating a Hanging Indent

40 Double-Spacing a Document

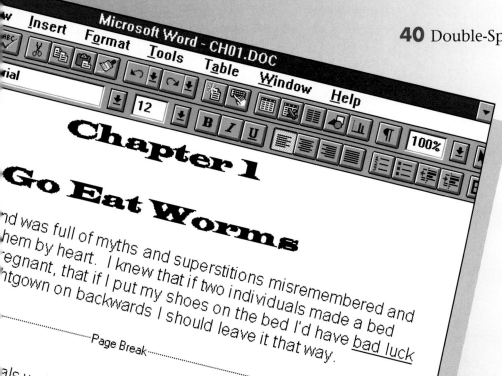

Formatting the document means you can change the appearance of text in your document. With Word for Windows' formatting tools, you can make your document more attractive and readable. In this part you learn how easy it is to boldface, italicize, underline text, change the font, change the font size, and center and right-align text. You also learn how to indent text, create a hanging indent, and double-space a document.

Making text boldface is one of the most common formatting changes you'll make in a document. Italics is another common formatting change. The Sample Documents (Part IX) section contains several documents that use boldface and italics.

The Underline command enables you to underline text in your document. To underline text, you can use the Format Font command and then choose from several underline styles in the Font dialog box. The Underline styles include single, words only, double, and dotted. In this part, you learn how to apply the underline style using the mouse.

A *font* is a style of type in a particular typeface and size. Word for Windows displays various fonts and font sizes in the Formatting toolbar. You can use the fonts provided by Word for Windows as well as fonts designed especially for your printer. If Word for Windows does not have a screen version of the printer font you select, it substitutes a font. In this case, the printout looks different than the screen.

You can apply fonts to a single word or any amount of text you want to change. You can also change the font size and font colors. The Font Color option in the Font dialog box let you change font colors easily. There are many font colors in various shades, hues, and patterns that you can choose to make your document more attractive. Of course, you must have a color monitor and a color printer to benefit from changing font colors.

Changing the font and the font size is an easy way to change the look and feel of your document. The Sample Documents (Part IX) section contains several documents that illustrate the effect of font changes.

You can align text left, center, right, or justified. The default alignment is Left. *Left alignment* means that text is aligned flush with the left margin. Center alignment centers text between the left and right margins. Right-aligned text appears flush with the right margin. Justified text spreads text between the left and right margins by expanding or contracting the space between words.

Left-aligned text appears "ragged right" on the page or column, which is warm and readable. Usually, left-alignment is used for conventional and office correspondence. Justified text, which has an orderly look, is generally used in multiple-column newsletters, newspapers, and magazines.

In this part, you learn how to center and right-align text. Also, the Sample Documents (Part IX) section contains a few documents that use center and right alignment. If you want to justify text, select the text you want to justify, and then simply click the Justify button on the Formatting toolbar.

Word for Windows provides another way to align paragraphs. You can indent paragraphs from the left, right, or both margins. You can also indent only the first line of the paragraph.

Normally, documents are single-spaced. However, Word for Windows enables you to change the line spacing in your documents. You can choose from Single, 1.5 lines, Double, At Least (the current point size), Exactly, and Multiple.

The At Least line spacing option specifies the minimum amount of space between lines. Word for Windows adds additional space as needed. The Exactly option specifies a fixed amount of space between lines. Word for Windows does not add additional space, even if needed. Multiple specifies an increased or decreased amount of space between lines (in points or lines).

The Sample Documents (Part IX) section contains a document that uses double-spacing.

Bold

Italic

<u>Underline</u>

Helvetica

Garamond

Shelley

American Typewriter

In this part, you learn some of the most important formatting operations you need for changing the appearance of your documents.

TASK 31
Making Text Bold

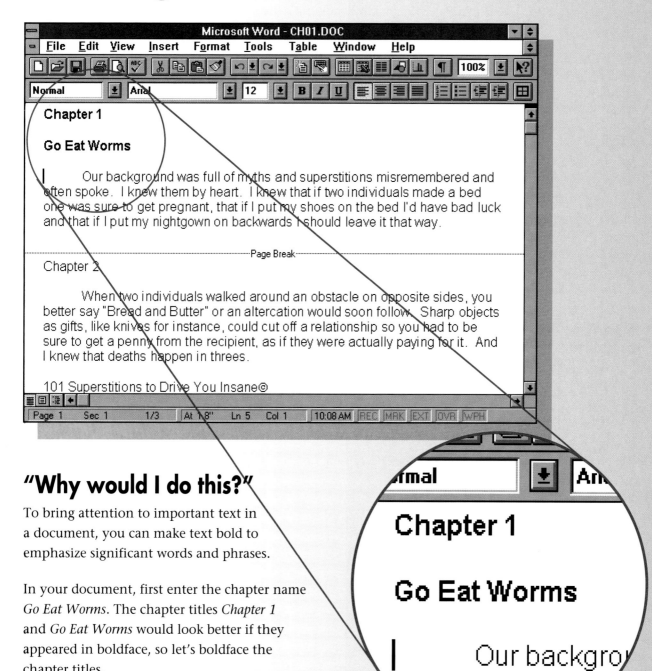

"Why would I do this?"

To bring attention to important text in
a document, you can make text bold to
emphasize significant words and phrases.

In your document, first enter the chapter name
Go Eat Worms. The chapter titles *Chapter 1*
and *Go Eat Worms* would look better if they
appeared in boldface, so let's boldface the
chapter titles.

1 Type **Go Eat Worms** below Chapter 1 and then press **Enter**. Next, click the left margin next to *Chapter 1* and drag down to the next line *Go Eat Worms*. This step selects the two lines of the text you want to make bold.

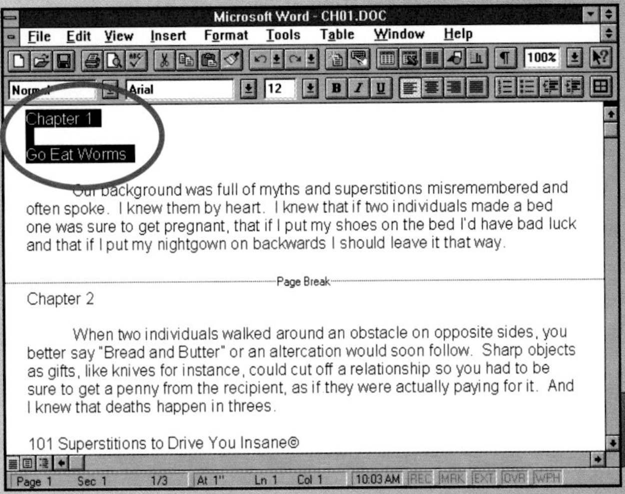

2 Click the **Bold** button in the Formatting toolbar. Clicking the Bold button applies bold to the selected text—in this case, the chapter titles.

NOTE

You can also press Ctrl+B to select the Bold command.

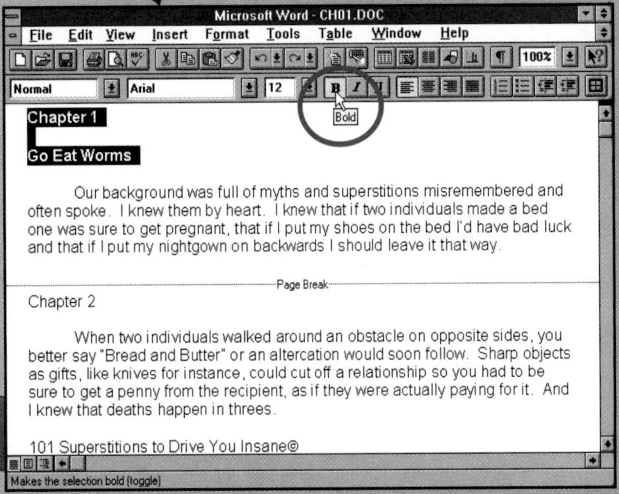

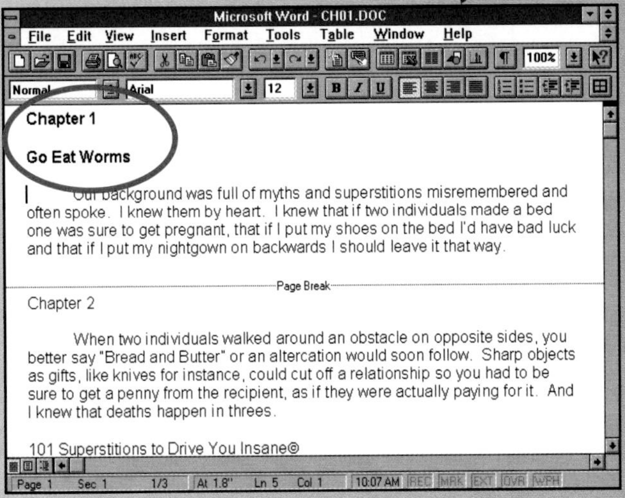

3 Click outside the selected text. This step deselects the text.

WHY WORRY?

To undo the bold, click the Undo button on the Standard toolbar immediately.

Italicizing Text

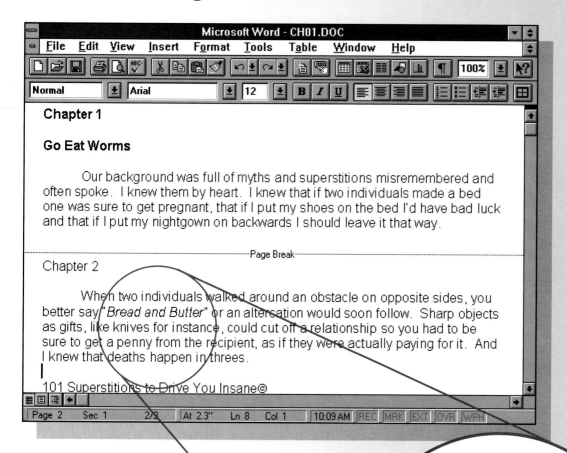

"Why would I do this?"

To enhance important words and phrases in a document, you can specify the italic style to make the text stand out in the document.

In your document, italicize the words "Bread and Butter" in the first sentence on page 2.

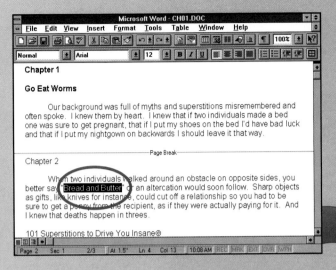

1 Click the left of the word *Bread* and drag to the word *Butter*. This step selects the text you want to italicize.

2 Click the **Italic** button on the Formatting toolbar. Clicking the Italic button italicizes the text—in this case, the words Bread and Butter.

NOTE ▼

You also can press Ctrl+I to select the Italic command.

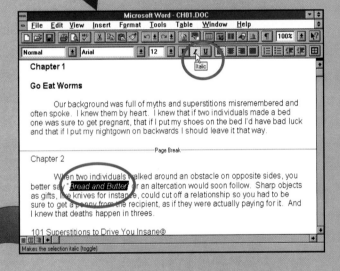

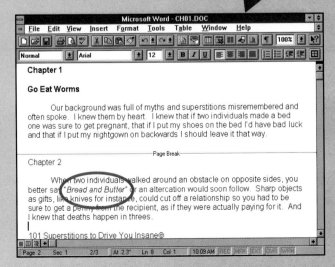

3 Click outside the selected text. This step deselects the text.

WHY WORRY?

To undo the italic font style, click the Undo button on the Standard toolbar immediately.

TASK 33
Underlining Text

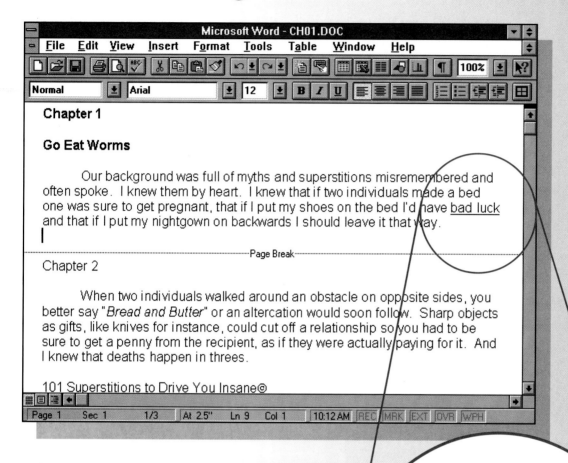

Microsoft Word - CH01.DOC

File   Edit   View   Insert   Format   Tools   Table   Window   Help

Normal   Arial   12   **B** *I* U

Chapter 1

Go Eat Worms

Our background was full of myths and superstitions misremembered and often spoke. I knew them by heart. I knew that if two individuals made a bed one was sure to get pregnant, that if I put my shoes on the bed I'd have <u>bad luck</u> and that if I put my nightgown on backwards I should leave it that way.

Page Break

Chapter 2

When two individuals walked around an obstacle on opposite sides, you better say "*Bread and Butter*" or an altercation would soon follow. Sharp objects as gifts, like knives for instance, could cut off a relationship so you had to be sure to get a penny from the recipient, as if they were actually paying for it. And I knew that deaths happen in threes.

101 Superstitions to Drive You Insane©

Page 1   Sec 1   1/3   At 2.5"   Ln 9   Col 1   10:12 AM   REC   MRK   EXT   OVR   WPH

mbered and
lade a bed
have <u>bad luck</u>
ray.

"Why would I do this?"

You can specify the underline style to emphasize significant words and phrases in your document.

In your document, underline the words *bad luck* in the last sentence on page 1.

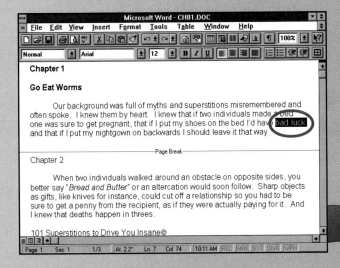

1 Click the left of the word *bad* and drag to the next word *luck*. This step selects the text you want to underline.

2 Click the **Underline** button on the Formatting toolbar. Clicking the Underline button underlines the text—in this case, bad luck.

NOTE ▼

You can also press Ctrl+U to select the Underline command.

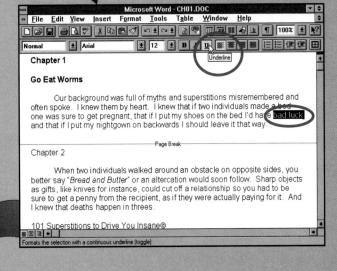

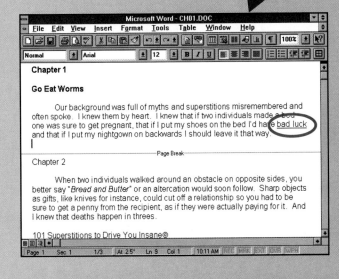

3 Click outside the selected text. This step deselects the text.

WHY WORRY?

To undo the underline font style, click the Undo button on the Standard toolbar immediately.

Changing the Font

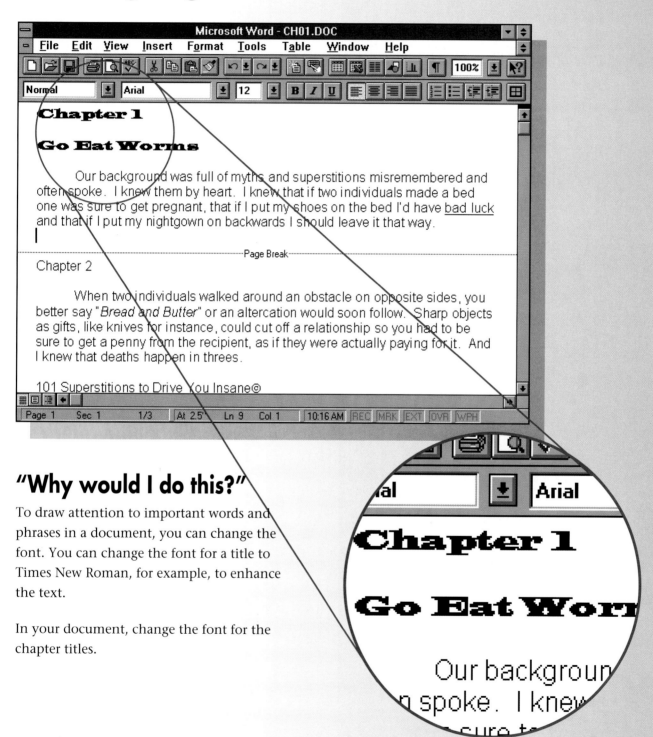

"Why would I do this?"

To draw attention to important words and phrases in a document, you can change the font. You can change the font for a title to Times New Roman, for example, to enhance the text.

In your document, change the font for the chapter titles.

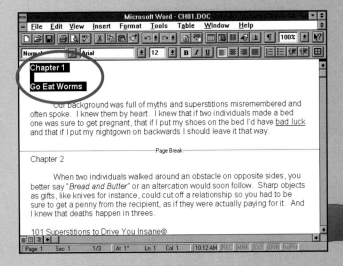

1 Click the left margin next to *Chapter 1* and drag down to the next line *Go Eat Worms*. This step selects the text you want to change.

2 Click the down arrow button next to the Font box on the Formatting toolbar. This step displays the list of fonts. Click on Wide Latin. This step changes the text to the font selected.

> **NOTE** ▼
>
> The fonts displayed in the list can vary, depending on the type of printer you have and the fonts installed.

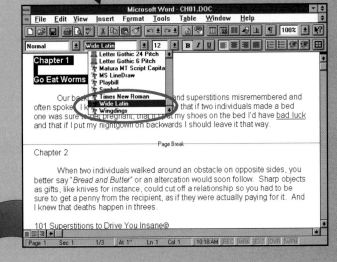

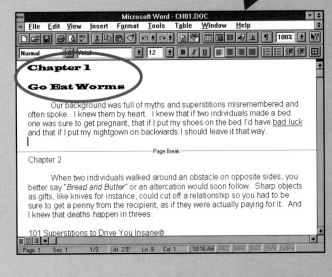

3 Click outside the selected text to deselect the text.

> **WHY WORRY?**
>
> To undo the font change, immediately click the Undo button on the Standard toolbar.

Changing the Font Size

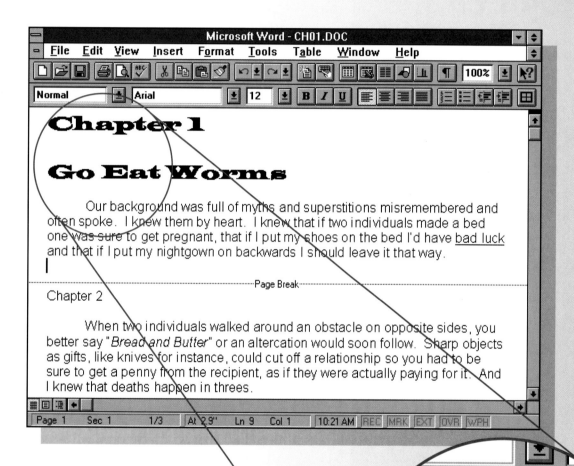

"Why would I do this?"

Changing the font size helps call attention to certain text within a document. You can change the font size to 24-point, for example, to make a title stand out at the top of the document.

In your document, change the font size for the chapter titles.

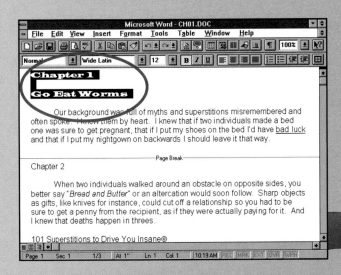

1 Click the left margin next to *Chapter 1* and drag down to the next line *Go Eat Worms*. This step selects the two lines of the text you want to change.

2 Click the **down arrow** button next to the Font Size box on the Formatting toolbar. This step displays the list of font sizes. Click a larger font size (a higher number); choose 18. This step changes the font size for the chapter titles.

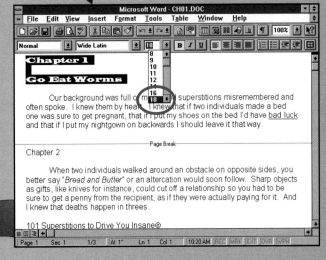

NOTE ▼

The font sizes in the list can vary, depending on the type of printer you have and the selected font.

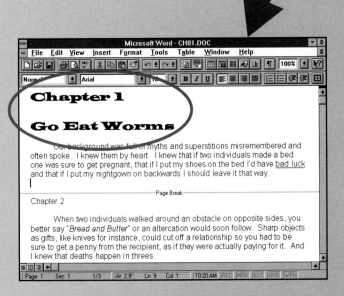

3 Click outside the selected text to deselect the text. The text appears bigger than it was before.

WHY WORRY?

To undo the font size change, immediately click the Undo button on the Standard toolbar.

TASK 36
Centering Text

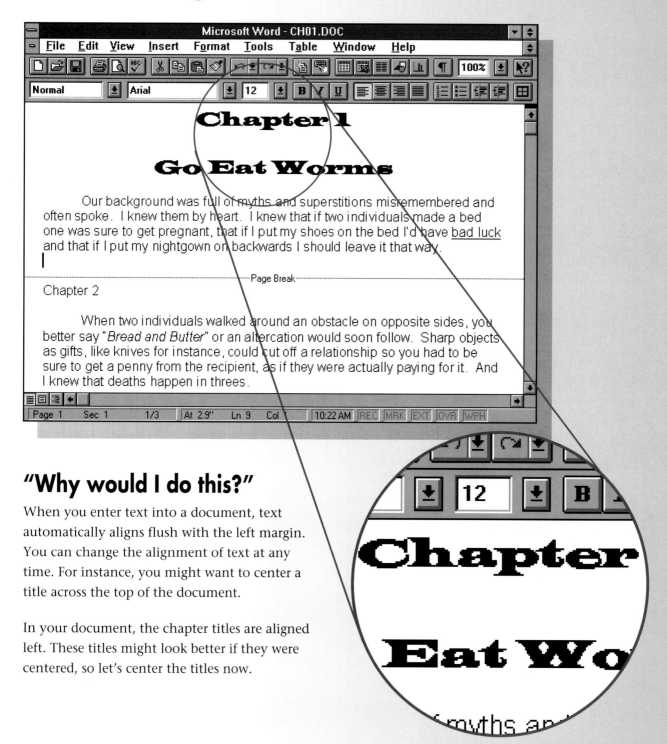

"Why would I do this?"

When you enter text into a document, text automatically aligns flush with the left margin. You can change the alignment of text at any time. For instance, you might want to center a title across the top of the document.

In your document, the chapter titles are aligned left. These titles might look better if they were centered, so let's center the titles now.

Task 36: Centering Text

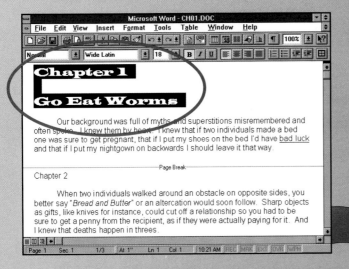

1 Click the left margin next to *Chapter 1* and drag down to the next line *Go Eat Worms*. This step selects the two lines of the text you want to center.

2 Click the **Center** button on the Formatting toolbar. This step selects the Center command. Word for Windows centers the text—in this case, the chapter titles.

NOTE ▼

You can also press Ctrl+E to center a line of text.

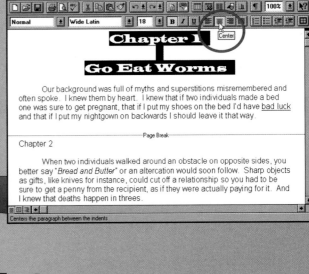

3 Click outside the selected text. This step deselects the text.

WHY WORRY?

To undo the most recent alignment change, immediately click the Undo button on the Standard toolbar.

TASK 37

Aligning Text Flush Right

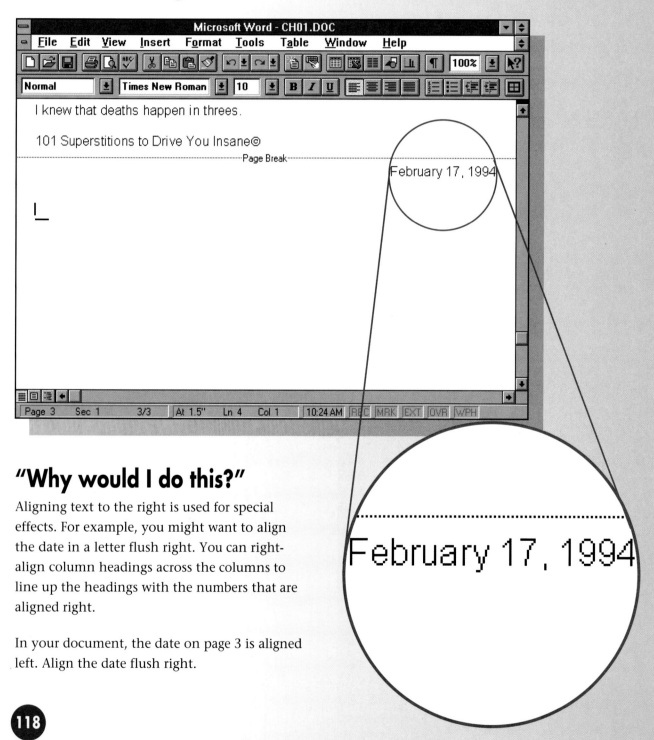

"Why would I do this?"

Aligning text to the right is used for special effects. For example, you might want to align the date in a letter flush right. You can right-align column headings across the columns to line up the headings with the numbers that are aligned right.

In your document, the date on page 3 is aligned left. Align the date flush right.

Task 37: Aligning Text Flush Right

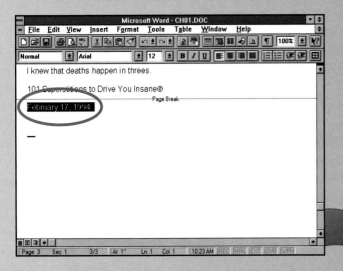

1 Press PgDn or scroll down to page 3. Then, click the left margin next to the date. This step selects the text you want to right-align.

2 Click the **Align Right** button on the Formatting toolbar. This step selects the Right alignment command. Word for Windows right-aligns the date.

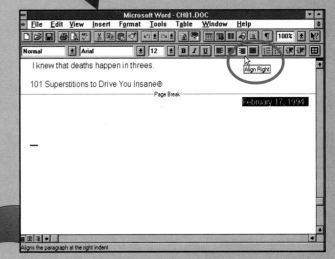

> **NOTE** ▼
>
> You can also press Ctrl+R to right-align a line of text.

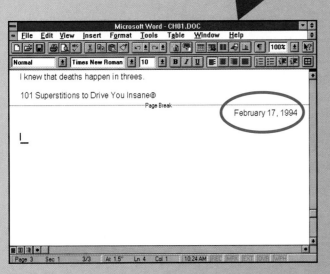

3 Click outside the selected text. This step deselects the text.

> **WHY WORRY?**
>
> To undo the most recent alignment change, immediately click the Undo button on the Standard toolbar.

TASK 38
Indenting Text

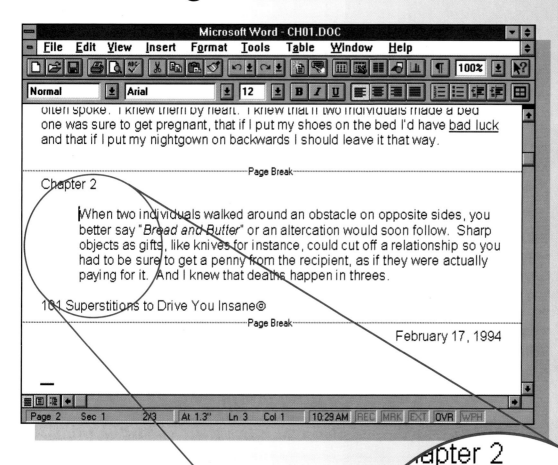

"Why would I do this?"

Another way to align paragraphs is to indent them relative to the margins. You can adjust the indents by specific measurements or by the Ruler. You might want to indent the entire paragraph to the right of the left margin to make the paragraph stand out from the rest of the paragraphs. For example, a contract may contain indented paragraphs.

In your document, first remove the tab preceding the paragraph on page 2. Then indent the entire paragraph on page 2 to the right of the left margin by 1/4 inch.

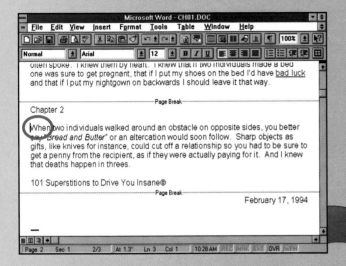

1 Click before the tab (blank space) in the paragraph on page 2. Then, press **Delete** to remove the tab. As you can see, the insertion point is already in the paragraph you want to indent.

2 Click the **Increase Indent** button on the Formatting toolbar. Clicking the Increase Indent button indents text 1/4 inch. As you can see, the paragraph is now indented.

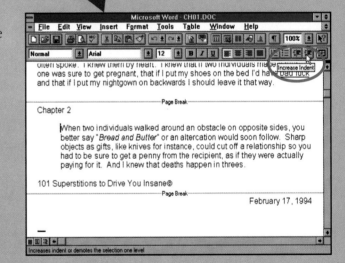

NOTE ▼

You can also press Ctrl+M to indent the current paragraph 1/4 inch. Press Ctrl+Shift+M to undo the indent.

WHY WORRY?

To undo the indent, click the Undo button on the Standard toolbar or the Decrease Indent button on the Formatting toolbar immediately.

TASK 39

Creating a Hanging Indent

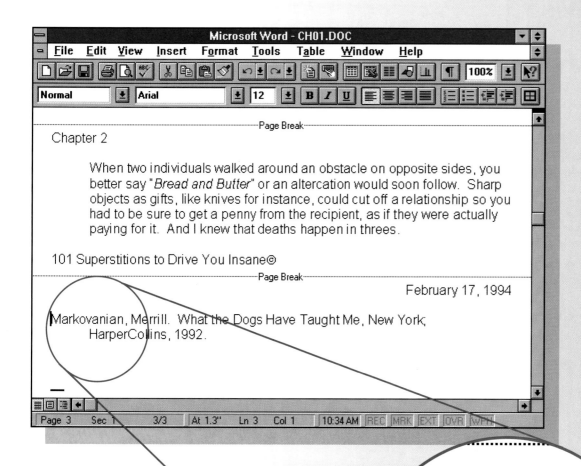

"Why would I do this?"

A *hanging indent* "hangs" the first line of a paragraph to the left of the rest of the paragraph. Hanging indents are useful for bulleted and numbered lists, glossary items, and bibliographic entries.

In your document, first type a bibliographic entry on page 3. Then, create a hanging indent for the paragraph.

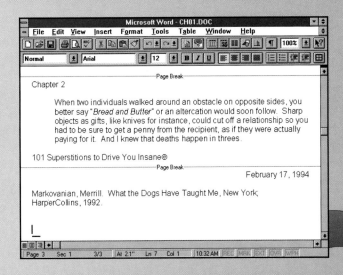

1 Click at the beginning of the line below the date on page 3, and then type **Markovanian, Merrill. What the Dogs Have Taught Me, New York; HarperCollins, 1992.** Press **Enter** twice.

2 Click before the *M* in *Markovanian*. This step places the insertion point where you want to indent text.

NOTE ▼

This task creates a hanging indent for one paragraph. You can also create hanging indents for several paragraphs at one time. To create hanging indents for more than one paragraph, select those paragraphs.

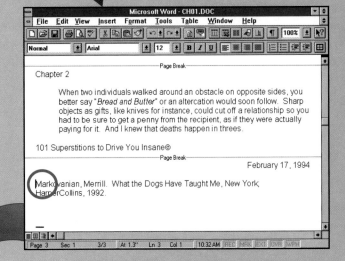

3 Click **Format** on the menu bar. Then, click **Paragraph**. This step selects the Format Paragraph command and displays the Paragraph dialog box. This dialog box has two tabs. The first tab, Indents and Spacing, controls the alignment and spacing.

Task 39: Creating a Hanging Indent

4 Click the down arrow next to the Special option. This step displays a list of special indent types.

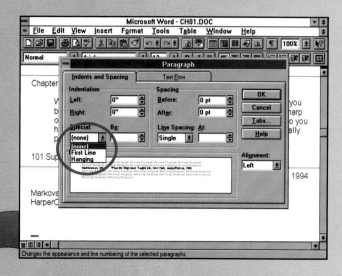

5 Click **Hanging**. This step selects a hanging indent. The amount to indent by (0.5") is filled in automatically. Click **OK**. This step confirms the choice and closes the dialog box.

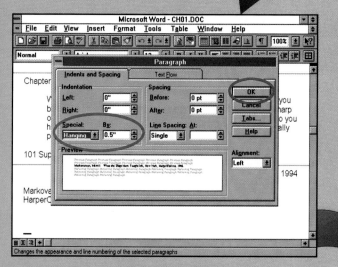

> **NOTE** ▼
>
> You can also press Ctrl+T to create a hanging indent. Press Ctrl+Shift+T to undo the hanging indent.

6 The first line of the paragraph is flush left, but the second line is indented 1/2 inch.

> **WHY WORRY?**
>
> To undo the hanging indent, click the Undo button on the Standard toolbar immediately.

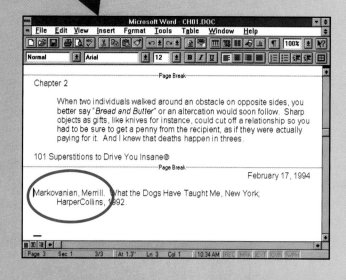

Double-Spacing a Document

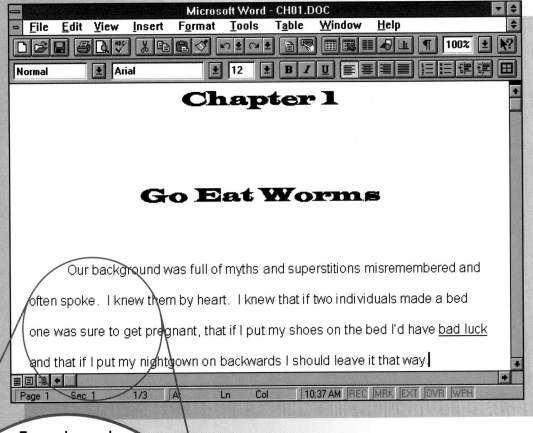

"Why would I do this?"

With Word for Windows, you can adjust line spacing to improve the appearance of a document. Most command-line spacing options include single-spacing (default), 1-1/2 lines, and double-spacing. For example, you might want to double-space a draft, a document, or a script so that you can mark your changes more easily on the printed pages.

In your document, double-space the text on page 1.

Task 40: Double-Spacing a Document

1 Press **Ctrl+Home** to move to the top of the document. Then, hold down the mouse button and drag the mouse to select all the text on page 1. This step selects the text you want to double-space.

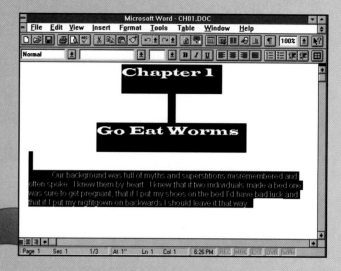

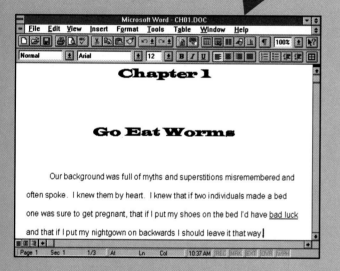

2 Press Ctrl+2. Pressing Ctrl+2 tells Word for Windows to double-space the selected text. As you can see, the selected text is double-spaced. Click outside the selected text to deselect the text.

WHY WORRY?

To undo the line spacing change, immediately click the Undo button on the Standard toolbar.

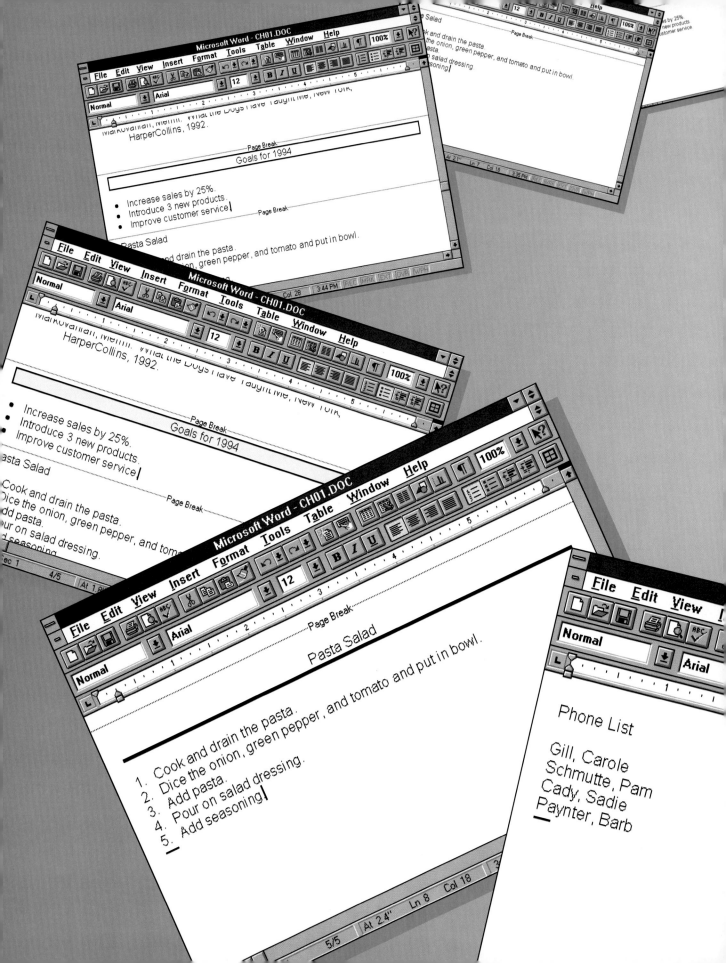

PART VI

More Formatting

41 Creating a Bulleted List

42 Creating a Numbered List

43 Adding a Border to a Paragraph

44 Shading a Paragraph

45 Adding a Line to a Paragraph

46 Setting a Default Tab

47 Setting Margins

48 Centering a Page

49 Numbering Pages

50 Creating Headers and Footers

51 Editing Headers and Footers

52 Inserting a Graphic

53 Moving and Resizing a Graphic

54 Deleting a Graphic

55 Creating a Table

56 Entering Text in a Table

57 Adding a Row to a Table

58 Deleting a Row from a Table

59 Creating a Two-Column Document

60 Inserting a WordArt Object

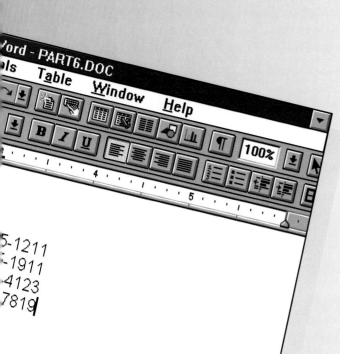

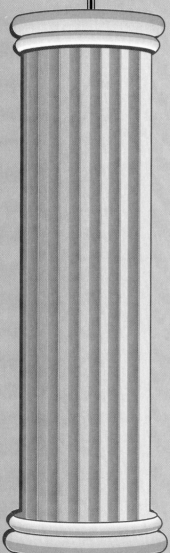

In this part, you learn how to create a bulleted list and a numbered list, add a border to a paragraph, shade a paragraph, and add a line to a paragraph. You also learn how to set a default tab, set margins, center a page, number pages, and create and edit headers and footers.

This part also shows you how to insert a graphic, move and resize a graphic, and delete a graphic. You also learn how to create a table, enter text in a table, add a row to a table, and delete a row from a table. Finally, you learn how to create a two-column document and insert a WordArt object.

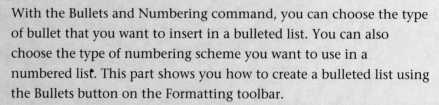

With the Bullets and Numbering command, you can choose the type of bullet that you want to insert in a bulleted list. You can also choose the type of numbering scheme you want to use in a numbered list. This part shows you how to create a bulleted list using the Bullets button on the Formatting toolbar.

To change the bullet type, choose the Format Bullets and Numbering command. Then click the Bulleted tab and choose the type of bullet you want. If you want to change the numbering scheme for a numbered list, choose the Format Bullets and Numbering command. Then click the Numbered tab and choose the type of numbering scheme you want.

One of the best ways to enhance the appearance of a document is to add borders to the text in the document. You can use the Borders button on the Formatting toolbar to add boxes around paragraphs, add emphasis lines anywhere in the document, and shade paragraphs. Adding a border, lines, and shading works for document headings or sections of a document that you want to set off. The Sample Documents section (Part IX) contains several documents that show off these features.

Adding lines works well on newsletters, as one example. Lines can also be used to separate parts of a document.

Setting tabs can be tricky. You choose the Format Tabs command and specify tab stops in the Tabs dialog box. In this part, you learn how easy it is to set a default tab stop for the entire document using the Ruler. You can also change the tab stops for just one paragraph.

When you choose the File Page Setup command, you see the Page Setup dialog box. The Page Setup dialog box contains four types of options: Margins, Paper

Size, Paper Source, and Layout. You can move from one set of options to another by clicking the appropriate tab in the Page Setup dialog box.

The Margins options in the Page Setup dialog box controls the top, bottom, left, and right margins. The Paper Size options control the paper size (width and height) of the paper you print on and the orientation. The default print orientation is Portrait, which means that the document prints vertically on the paper. You can choose Landscape to print the document sideways or horizontally on the paper. If the document is too wide, you can try moving some text if possible.

If the document is still too large to print on one page, you can change the top, bottom, left, and right margins. You also might consider reducing the printout using the Shrink to Fit option in the Print Preview screen. This option offers the ability to remove orphans and widows—to eliminate lagging single lines on a page. See Part VII, Viewing and Printing Documents, for more information on the Print Preview command.

The Paper Source options tell Word for Windows whether your printer feeds paper with a paper tray or a sheet feeder. The Layout options include options for sections, headers and footers, vertical alignment, and line numbers. It is a good idea to experiment with all the page setup options until you get the results you want.

When you add page numbers with the Insert Page Numbers command, you add them to a header or footer. You can specify whether to add the page numbers to the top of each page (to a header) or to the bottom of each page (to a footer). You can also specify the alignment.

Word lets you add headers and footers to print information at the top and bottom of every page of the printout. You can create your own header and footer information and you can include any text plus special commands to control the appearance of the header or footer.

You can insert graphics to spice up your document, create a table to easily and quickly enter text and numbers (similar to a spreadsheet), and create a two-column document for newspaper, newsletter, and magazine articles.

This part shows you formatting operations you need for enhancing the appearance and layout of your documents.

Creating a Bulleted List

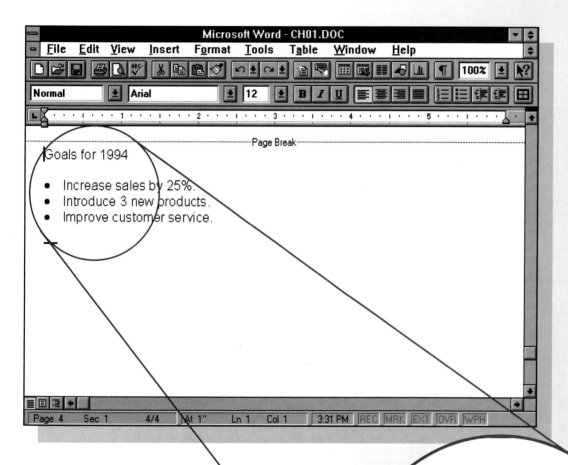

"Why would I do this?"

Bulleted lists are good when you want to present a series of ideas. The list helps the readers visually follow along. For example, you can create a bulleted list for goals, an agenda, an overhead slide, or a list of key points you want to cover at a meeting.

In your document, move to the bottom of the document and create a new page. Then, type a list containing three items. Finally, add bullets to the items in the list.

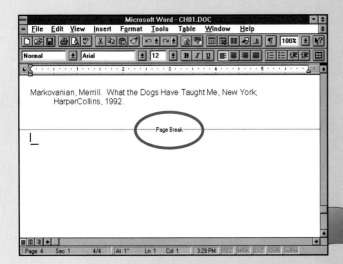

1 Press **Ctrl+End** or scroll to the bottom of the document. Then, press **Ctrl+Enter** to insert a page break.

2 On page 4, type the text that appears in the figure so that your computer screen matches the screen in the book.

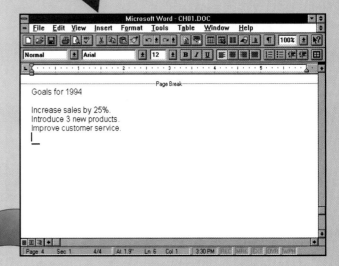

3 Select all of the paragraphs, except the first one. This step selects the text to which you want to add bullets.

Task 41: Creating a Bulleted List

4 Click the **Bullets** button on the Formatting toolbar. Clicking the Bullets button creates a bulleted list.

5 Click outside the selected text. This step deselects the text. Now you can see the bulleted list better.

WHY WORRY?

To remove the bullets in the list, immediately click the Undo button on the Standard toolbar.

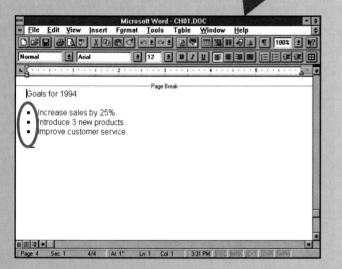

Creating a Numbered List

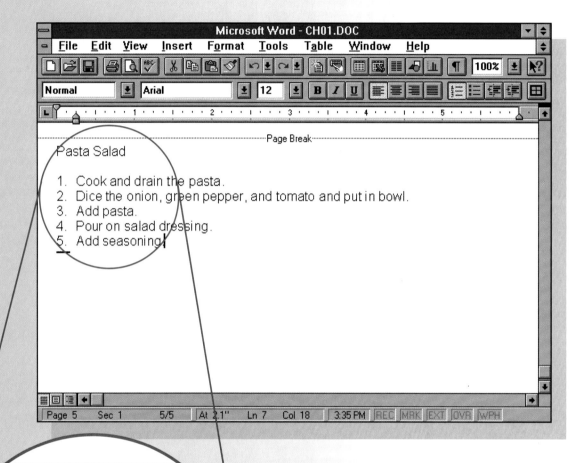

"Why would I do this?"

Numbered lists are good when you want to present a series of ideas. The list helps the readers visually follow along. For example, you can create a numbered list for a set of instructions, a recipe, or a list of key points you want to cover at a meeting.

In your document, move to the bottom of the document and create a new page. Then type a list containing five items. Finally, add numbers to the items in the list.

Task 42: Creating a Numbered List

1 Press **Ctrl+End** or scroll to the bottom of the document. Then, press **Ctrl+Enter** to insert a page break.

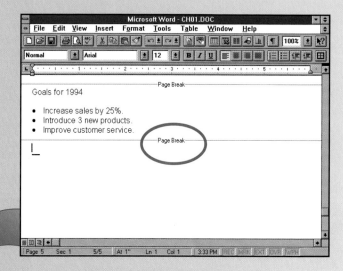

2 On page 5, type the text that appears in the figure so that your computer screen matches the screen in the book.

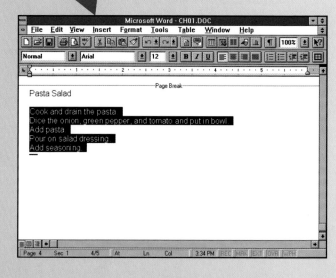

3 Select all of the paragraphs, except the first one. This step selects the text to which you want to add numbers.

4 Click the **Numbering** button on the Formatting toolbar. Clicking the Numbering button creates a numbered list.

5 Click outside the selected text. This step deselects the text. Now you can see the numbered list better.

WHY WORRY?

To remove the numbers in the list, immediately click the Undo button on the Standard toolbar.

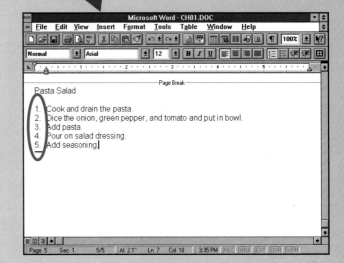

Adding a Border to a Paragraph

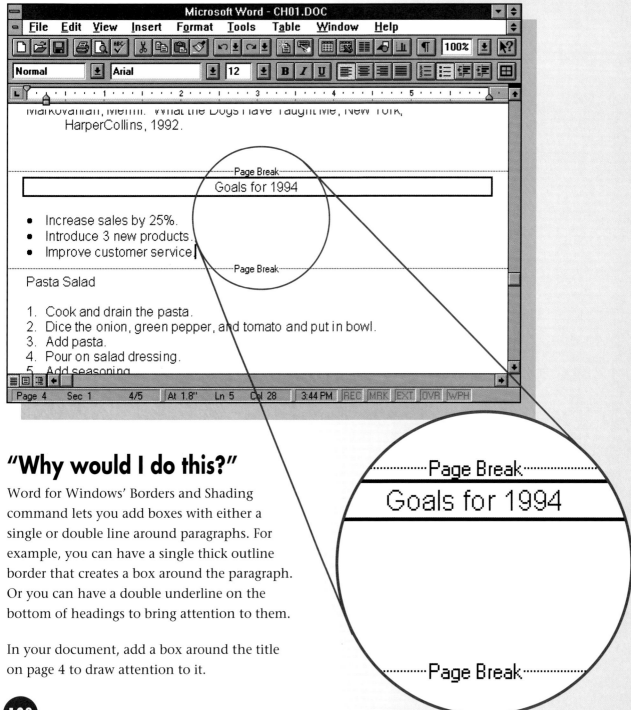

"Why would I do this?"

Word for Windows' Borders and Shading command lets you add boxes with either a single or double line around paragraphs. For example, you can have a single thick outline border that creates a box around the paragraph. Or you can have a double underline on the bottom of headings to bring attention to them.

In your document, add a box around the title on page 4 to draw attention to it.

Task 43: Adding a Border to a Paragraph

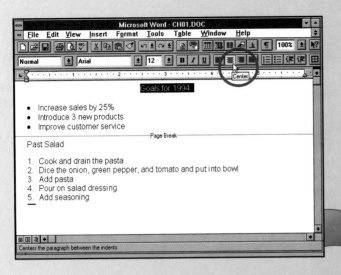

1 Press **PgUp** or scroll up to move to page 4. Select the title *Goals for 1994*. Click the **Center** button on the Standard toolbar to center the text. Leave the text selected so you can add a border to it.

2 Click the **Borders** button (the button with a thick border and four squares inside the border) on the Formatting toolbar. Clicking the Borders button displays the Borders toolbar below the Formatting toolbar. The Borders toolbar contains the Line Style list, border samples, and the Shading list.

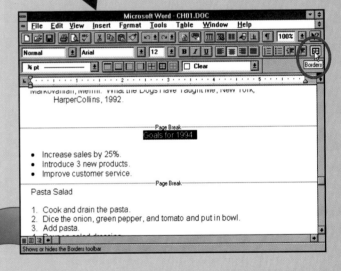

3 Click the **down arrow** in the Line Style list on the Borders toolbar. A list of line styles appears. Then, click **1 1/2 pt** in the Line Style list. This step tells Word for Windows what line style you want to use for the border.

Task 43: Adding a Border to a Paragraph

4 Click the **Outside Border** button (the button with a thick border with two dotted lines that look like four squares inside the box) on the Borders toolbar. This step tells Word for Windows to outline the edges of the paragraph with a single line.

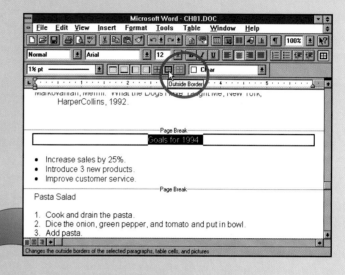

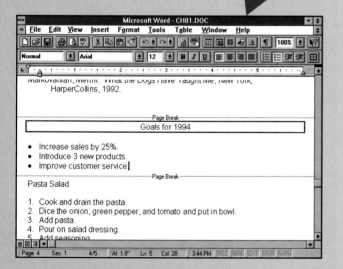

5 Click the **Borders** button on the Formatting toolbar. Clicking the Borders button again hides the Borders toolbar. Then, click outside the selected text. This step deselects the text so you can see the outline better.

WHY WORRY?

To remove the border, immediately click the Undo button on the Standard toolbar.

Shading a Paragraph

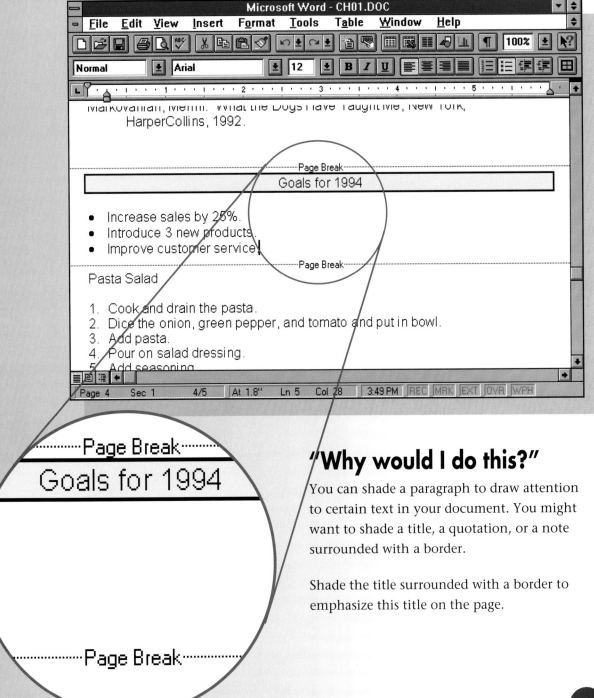

"Why would I do this?"

You can shade a paragraph to draw attention to certain text in your document. You might want to shade a title, a quotation, or a note surrounded with a border.

Shade the title surrounded with a border to emphasize this title on the page.

Task 44: Shading a Paragraph

1 Select the title *Goals for 1994*. This is the paragraph you want to shade.

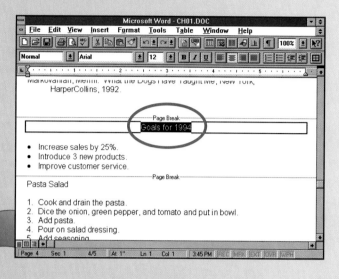

2 Click the **Borders** button (the button with a thick border and four squares inside the border) on the Formatting toolbar. Clicking the Borders button displays the Borders toolbar below the Formatting toolbar. The Borders toolbar contains the Line Style list, border samples, and the Shading list.

3 Click the **down arrow** in the Shading list on the Borders toolbar. A list of shading patterns appear. Then, click **10%** in the Shading list. This step tells Word for Windows the amount of shading you want.

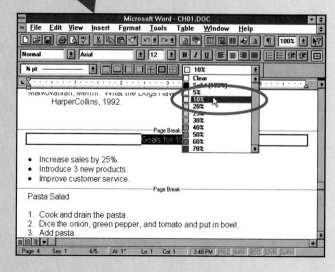

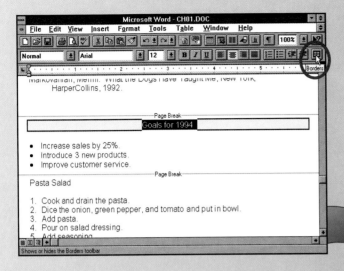

4 Click the **Borders** button on the Formatting toolbar. Clicking the Borders button again hides the Borders toolbar.

5 Click outside the selected text. This step deselects the text so you can see the shading better.

NOTE ▼

Depending on your printer, the shading might print differently than it appears on-screen, or not at all.

WHY WORRY?

To remove the shading, immediately click the Undo button on the Standard toolbar.

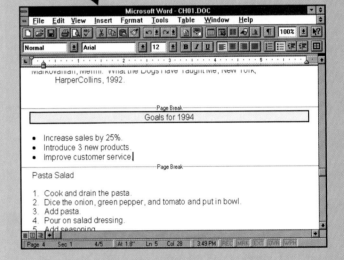

TASK 45
Adding a Line to a Paragraph

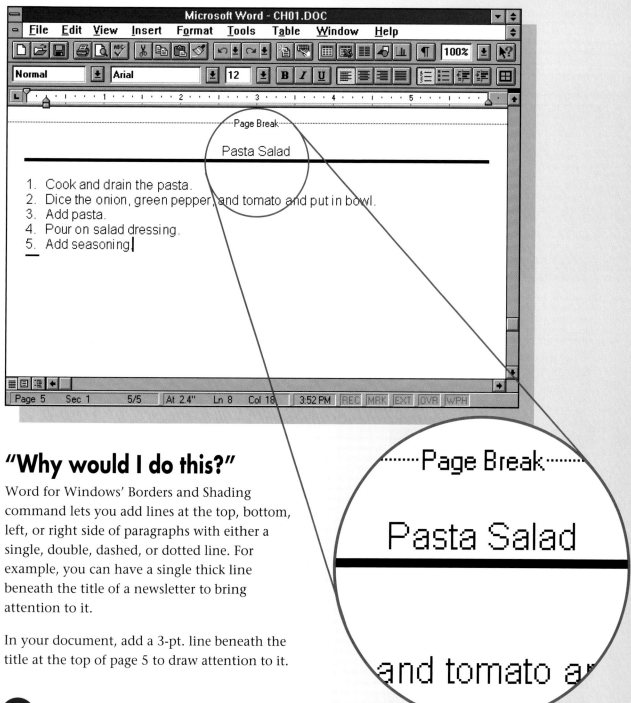

"Why would I do this?"

Word for Windows' Borders and Shading command lets you add lines at the top, bottom, left, or right side of paragraphs with either a single, double, dashed, or dotted line. For example, you can have a single thick line beneath the title of a newsletter to bring attention to it.

In your document, add a 3-pt. line beneath the title at the top of page 5 to draw attention to it.

Task 45: Adding a Line to a Paragraph

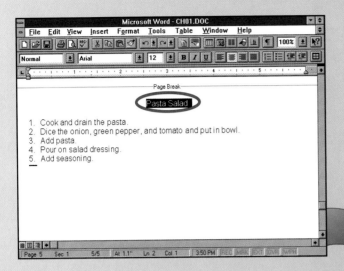

1 Press **PgDn** or scroll down to move to page 5. Select the title *Pasta Salad*. Click the **Center** button on the Standard toolbar to center the text. Leave the text selected so that you can add a bottom border to it.

2 Click the **Borders** button (the button with a thick border and four squares inside the border) on the Formatting toolbar. Clicking the Borders button displays the Borders toolbar below the Formatting toolbar. The Borders toolbar contains the Line Style list, border samples, and the Shading list.

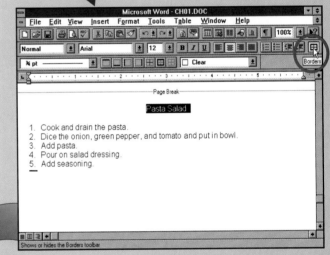

3 Click the **down arrow** in the Line Style list on the Borders toolbar. A list of line styles appears. Then, click **3 pt** in the Line Style list. This step tells Word for Windows what line style you want to use for the border.

Task 45: Adding a Line to a Paragraph

4 Click the **Bottom Border** button (the button with a thick border at the bottom of the dotted line paragraph) on the Borders toolbar. This step tells Word for Windows where to place the line.

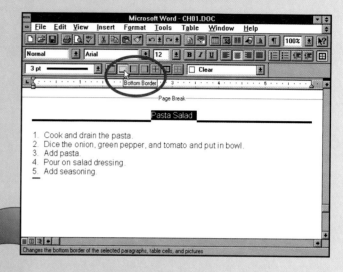

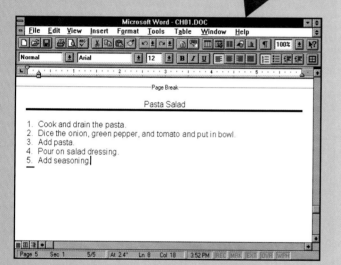

5 Click the **Borders** button on the Formatting toolbar. Clicking the Borders button again hides the Borders toolbar. Then, click outside the selected text. This step deselects the text so you can see the line better.

WHY WORRY?

To remove the line, immediately click the Undo button on the Standard toolbar.

Setting a Default Tab

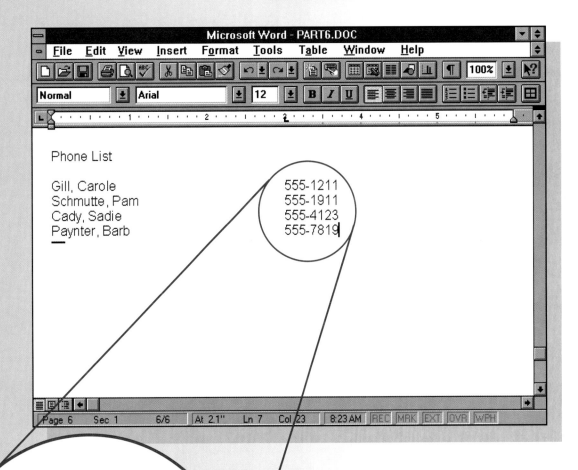

"Why would I do this?"

You can set different types of tab stops—left (default), right, decimal, or center tabs. You can also insert a dot leader before a tab stop. Setting a default tab is useful for creating a table that contains one or more columns.

First, type the text for a two-column table. Next, display the ruler, and set a default tab for the second column.

Task 46: Setting a Default Tab

1 Press **Ctrl+End** or scroll to the bottom of the document. Then, press **Ctrl+Enter** to insert a page break. On page 6, type the text that appears in the figure so that your computer screen matches the screen in the book. Be sure to press Tab after typing each name in the list.

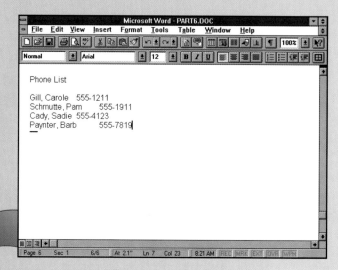

2 Click the left margin next to the first name, *Gill, Carole* and drag down to select the rest of the text. This step selects all the text except for the title. You want to set a default tab for the entire table.

3 Click **View** on the menu bar. Then, click **Ruler** to select View Ruler. Word either displays or hides the Ruler. At the left edge of the rule is the Tab Type button with the letter **L** on it, which stands for Left tab. You want to set a left tab.

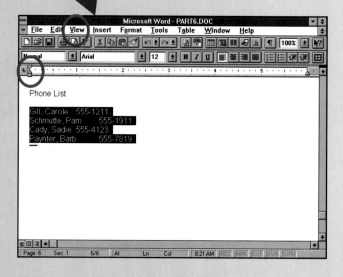

> **NOTE** ▼
>
> Click the Tab Type button to choose the type of tab stop—left (default), center, right, and decimal tabs.

4 Click beneath the number **3** on the Ruler. Clicking the **3** on the Ruler inserts a tab marker under the number 3. (Tab markers are symbols shaped like a letter L.) This step sets a default tab 3 inches from the left margin.

5 Click outside the selected text. This step deselects the text so that you can see the columns better.

WHY WORRY?

If you want to remove the default tab stop, select the text for which you set the default tab, click on the tab marker and holding the left mouse button down, drag it down off the Ruler. Then start over, or drag the tab marker to a new location on the Ruler.

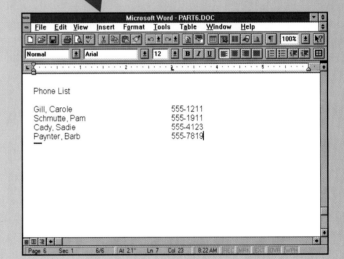

Setting Margins

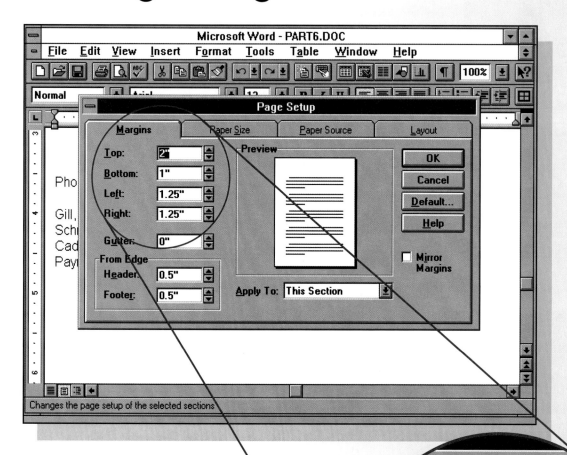

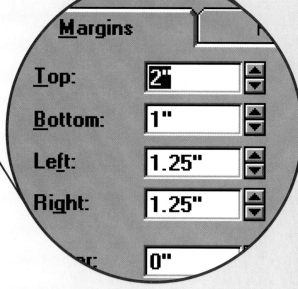

"Why would I do this?"

You can adjust the top, bottom, left, and right margins. You might want to change the margin settings for either the entire document, or for the document pages from the current position of the insertion point. Margins can also be changed for a single paragraph or a single page.

Let's set a 2-inch top margin for the entire document now.

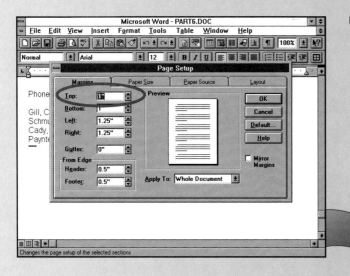

1 Click **File** on the menu bar. Then, click **Page Setup**. This step selects the File Page Setup command. You see the Page Setup dialog box. This dialog box includes four tabs: Margins, Paper Size, Paper Source, and Layout. By default, Margins is displayed. You see text boxes for each of the four margins: Top, Bottom, Left, and Right. The top entry is selected.

2 Type **2**. This step specifies a 2-inch top margin.

> **NOTE** ▼
>
> The default margins are 1 inch for the top and bottom and 1.25 inches for the left and right.

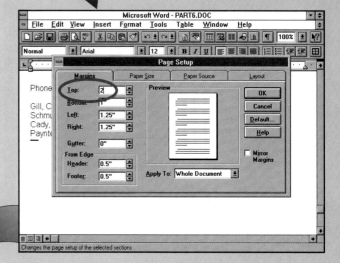

3 Click **OK**. This step confirms the new margin settings and closes the dialog box. To see the effect of the margin changes, you must preview the document.

> **WHY WORRY?**
>
> To cancel the margin change, click Cancel in the Page Setup dialog box. Or immediately click the Undo button on the Standard toolbar.

Centering a Page

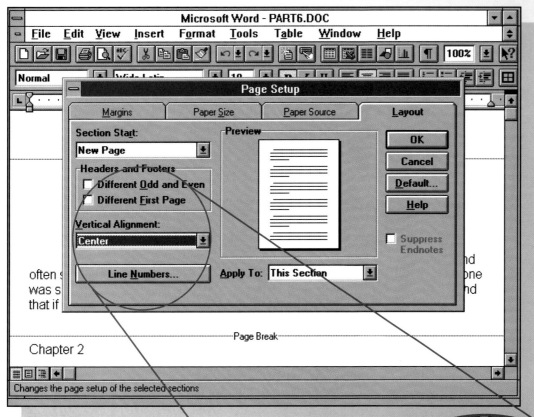

Microsoft Word - PART6.DOC

File   Edit   View   Insert   Format   Tools   Table   Window   Help

Normal

Page Setup

Margins   Paper Size   Paper Source   Layout

Section Start:
New Page

Headers and Footers
☐ Different Odd and Even
☐ Different First Page

Vertical Alignment:
Center

Line Numbers...

Preview

OK
Cancel
Default...
Help

☐ Suppress
Endnotes

Apply To: This Section

often s
was s
that if

Page Break

Chapter 2

Changes the page setup of the selected sections

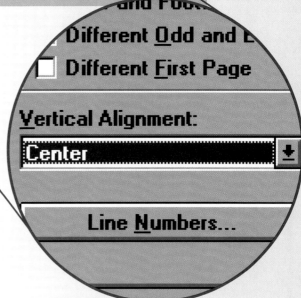

and Foo
Different Odd and E
☐ Different First Page

Vertical Alignment:
Center

Line Numbers...

"Why would I do this?"

Word for Windows' Vertical Alignment
command enables you to center the text on the
page vertically. You can align the text between
the top and bottom margins. Centering a page
works well for special documents such as an
invitation. Letters often look better on the page
when they are centered. Document, chapter, or
report titles look better on a title page when
they are centered.

Type the title on a separate page for your
document. Then, vertically center the title
on the title page.

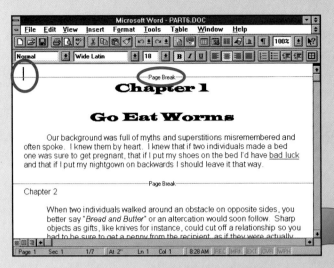

1 Press **Ctrl+Home** or scroll to the top of the document. Then, press **Ctrl+Enter** to insert a page break. Next, press the Up arrow key (↑) to move the insertion point to page 1.

2 Click the **Center** button on the Formatting toolbar to center the text you will type. Type **101 Superstitions** and press **Enter**; then type **to Drive You Insane**.

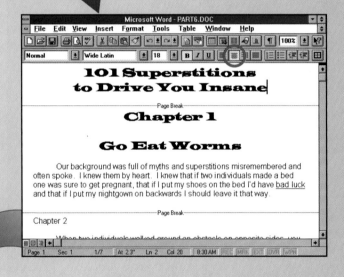

3 Click **File** on the menu bar and click **Page Setup**. Then, click the **Layout** tab to display the Layout options. This step selects the File Page Setup command. Word opens the Page Setup dialog box. Notice the layout options in the box.

Task 48: Centering a Page

4 Click the **down arrow** next to the **Vertical Alignment** option. This step displays a drop-down list of alignment choices.

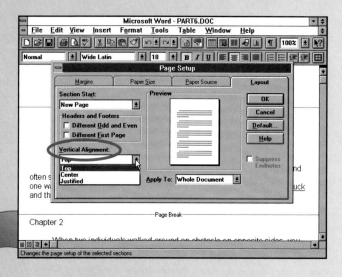

5 Click **Center**. This step tells Word for Windows to center the current page.

6 Click **OK**. Word for Windows closes the Page Setup dialog box. On-screen, you cannot see the vertical alignment change. To do so, you must preview the document.

WHY WORRY?

To cancel the vertical alignment change, click Cancel in the Page Setup dialog box. Or immediately click the Undo button on the Standard toolbar =.

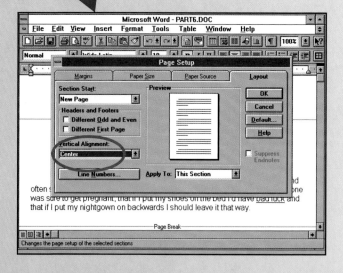

Numbering Pages

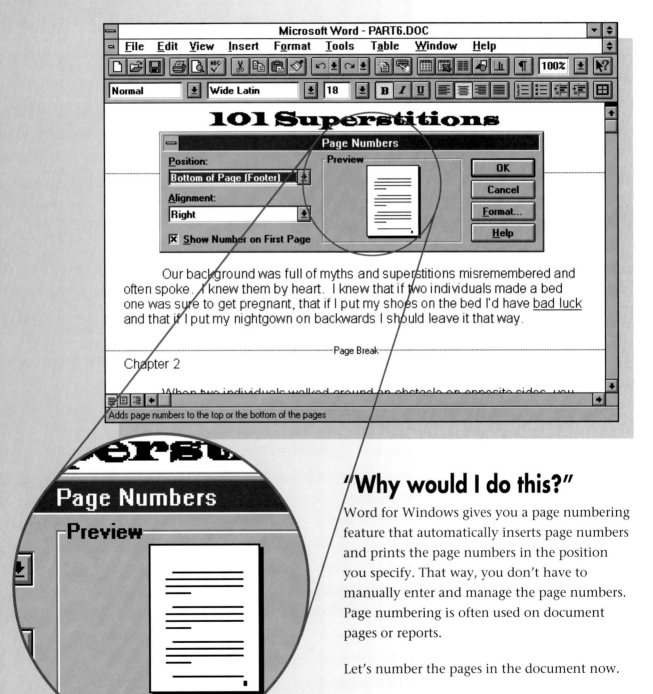

"Why would I do this?"

Word for Windows gives you a page numbering feature that automatically inserts page numbers and prints the page numbers in the position you specify. That way, you don't have to manually enter and manage the page numbers. Page numbering is often used on document pages or reports.

Let's number the pages in the document now.

Task 49: Numbering Pages

1 Click **Insert** on the menu bar. Then, click **Page Numbers**. This step selects the Insert Page Numbers command. Word opens the Page Numbers dialog box. The Page Numbers options appear in the dialog box. The default position is Bottom of Page (footer) and the default alignment is right.

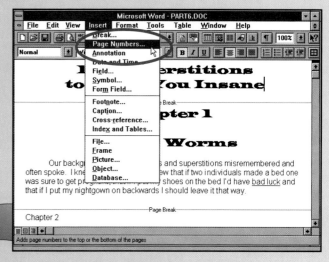

2 Click **OK**. This accepts the default. Word for Windows creates a footer and adds the right-aligned page number to the footer. On-screen, you cannot see the page numbers. To do so, you must preview the document or change the view to Page Layout.

NOTE ▼

If you don't want a page number on the first page, click in the Show Numbers on First Page check box so that there isn't an X in the box.

WHY WORRY?

If you change your mind, click Cancel in the Page Numbers dialog box. Or click the Undo button on the Standard toolbar immediately.

Creating Headers and Footers

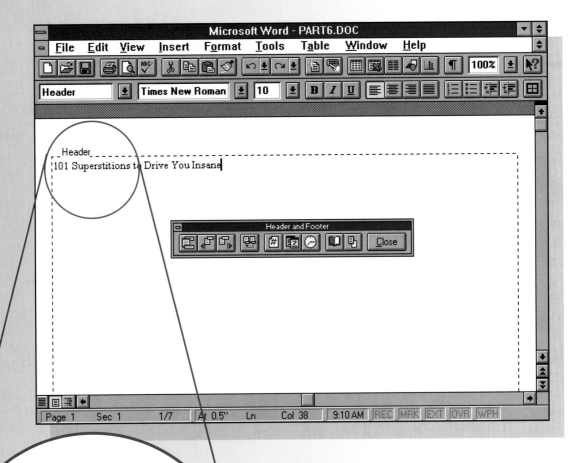

"Why would I do this?"

Headers and footers are lines of text that you can print at the top and bottom of every page in a print job—headers at the top, footers at the bottom. You can include any text, page numbers, the current date and time, and even format the information in a header and footer.

Create a header that contains the document title and a footer that contains the date in your document.

Task 50: Creating Headers and Footers

1 Click **View** on the menu bar. Then, click **Header and Footer**. This step selects the View Header and Footer command. Word displays the Header and Footer areas on-screen. You also see the Header and Footer toolbar. If the toolbar is interfering, you can click the toolbar and move it to a different location.

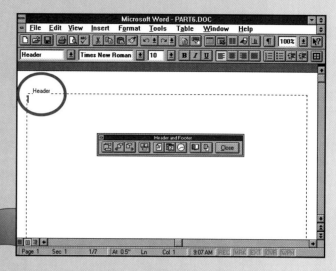

2 Type **101 Superstitions to Drive You Insane** in the Header area. This is the text you want to print at the top of each page.

3 Click the **Switch Between Header and Footer** button (the button with a piece of paper with a header at the top of the paper and a footer at the bottom of the paper) on the Header and Footer toolbar. Clicking the **Switch Between Header and Footer** button moves the insertion point to the Footer area.

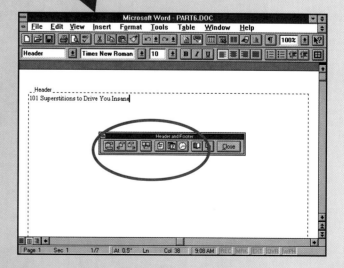

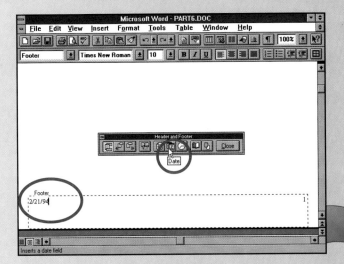

4 Click the **Date** button (the button with two calendar pages) on the Header and Footer toolbar. Clicking the **Date** button inserts the current date into the Footer area. This is the text you want to print at the bottom of each page.

NOTE ▼

You can also insert the page number. Word provides several header and footer options, such as formatting the header or footer text.

5 Click **Close** in the Header and Footer toolbar. This step confirms the header and footer and closes the Footer window. On-screen, you cannot see the header and footer. To do so, you must preview the document or switch the view to Page Layout.

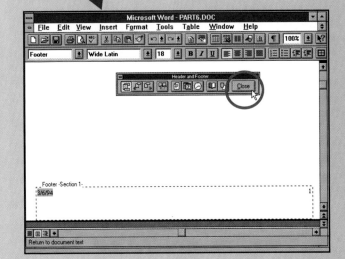

WHY WORRY?

If something unexpected prints at the top or bottom of your document, check the Header or Footer area. If you don't want a header or footer, select all the text in the Header or Footer area, and then press Delete to delete the header or footer.

Editing Headers and Footers

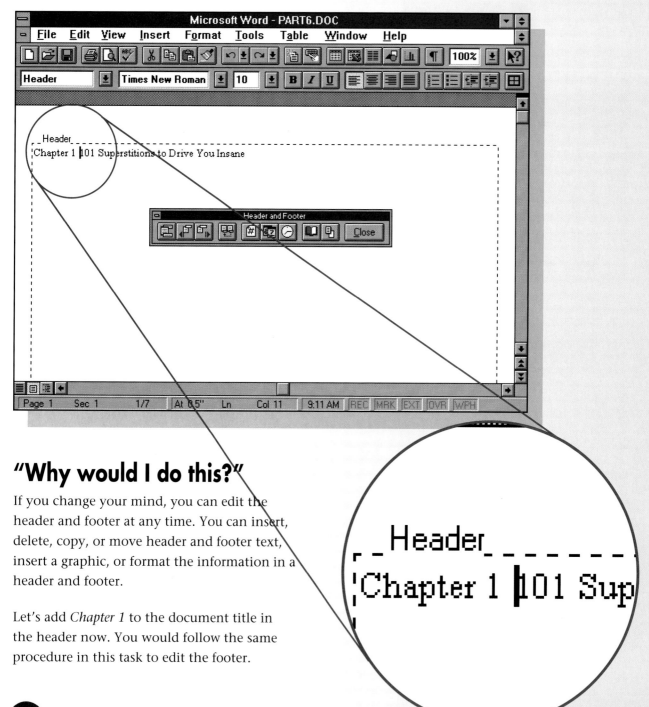

"Why would I do this?"

If you change your mind, you can edit the header and footer at any time. You can insert, delete, copy, or move header and footer text, insert a graphic, or format the information in a header and footer.

Let's add *Chapter 1* to the document title in the header now. You would follow the same procedure in this task to edit the footer.

Task 51: Editing Headers and Footers

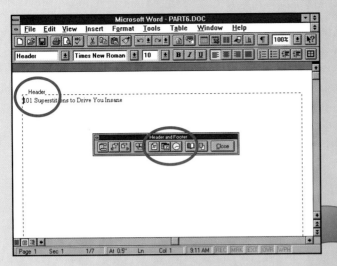

1 Click **View** on the menu bar. Then, click **Header and Footer**. This step selects the View Header and Footer command. Word displays the Header and Footer areas on-screen. You also see the Header and Footer toolbar.

2 Type **Chapter 1** in the Header area. Then, press the **space bar**. This is the additional text you want to print at the top of each page. Pressing the space bar inserts a space between the new text and the original text.

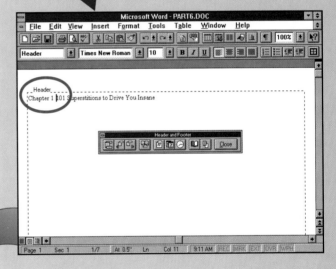

3 Click **Close** in the Header and Footer toolbar. This step confirms the header and closes the Header window. On-screen, you cannot see the header change. To do so, you must preview the document or switch to Page Layout view.

WHY WORRY?

Follow the same procedure to change the header back to its original text.

161

TASK 52
Inserting a Graphic

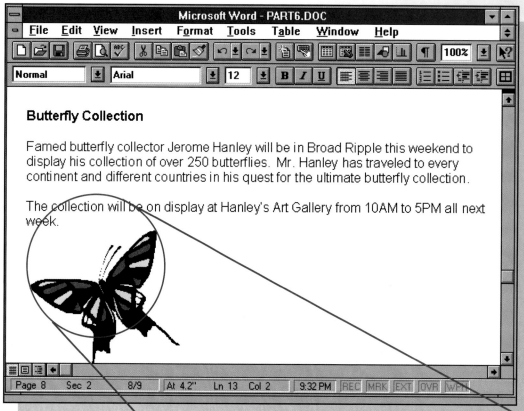

"Why would I do this?"

Word for Windows lets you insert graphics in your document to add emphasis and visual impact. Graphics can liven up any document.

Type a newsletter article about a butterfly collection, then insert a graphic of a butterfly below the article.

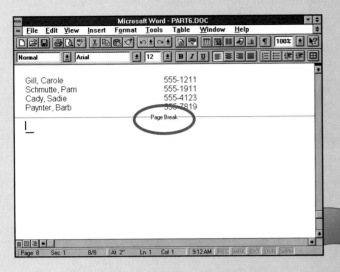

1 Press **Ctrl+End** or scroll to the bottom of the document. Then, press **Ctrl+Enter** to insert a page break.

2 On page 8, type the text that appears in the figure so that your computer screen matches the screen in the book.

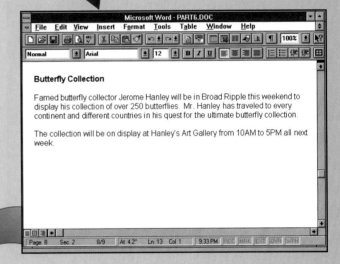

3 Click **Insert** on the menu bar. Then, click **Picture**. This step selects the Insert **Picture** command. Word opens the Insert **Picture** dialog box. The files in the CLIPART directory are displayed. Word for Windows comes with several clip-art images that you can insert in your document.

4 In the files list, click **butterfly.wmf**. This step selects the graphic that you want to insert.

NOTE ▼

To preview the graphic before you insert it, click the Preview Graphic check box in the Insert Graphic dialog box.

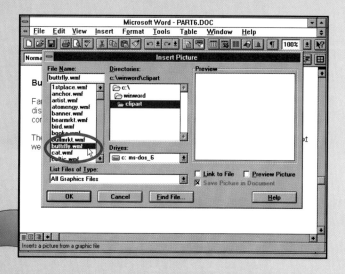

5 Click **OK**. The graphic is inserted on-screen in the default position and size. You can change the box position and size. See the next task.

NOTE ▼

Graphics are treated as characters when inserted this way. For more flexibility, create a frame and then insert the graphic.

WHY WORRY?

To undo the graphic insertion, click the Undo button on the Standard toolbar immediately.

Moving and Resizing a Graphic

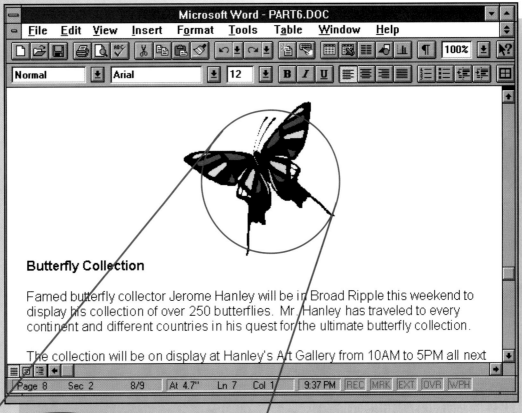

Microsoft Word - PART6.DOC

File   Edit   View   Insert   Format   Tools   Table   Window   Help

Normal   Arial   12   B I U

Butterfly Collection

Famed butterfly collector Jerome Hanley will be in Broad Ripple this weekend to display his collection of over 250 butterflies. Mr. Hanley has traveled to every continent and different countries in his quest for the ultimate butterfly collection.

The collection will be on display at Hanley's Art Gallery from 10AM to 5PM all next

Page 8   Sec 2   8/9   At 4.7"   Ln 7   Col 1   9:37 PM   REC   MRK   EXT   OVR   WPH

"Why would I do this?"

Once you've inserted a graphic in your document, you may need to move or resize it. If you want to shrink the graphic or make it taller and wider, you can move and resize it.

First move the butterfly to the top of the page, and then resize the butterfly, shrinking its height and width.

Task 53: Moving and Resizing a Graphic

1 Click the graphic. This step selects the graphic that you want to move. Selection handles appear around the sides of the graphic. Handles are the solid boxes at the corners and sides of the frame.

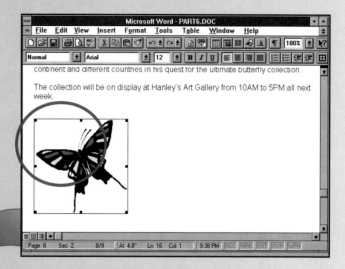

2 Click and hold down the mouse button and drag the graphic to the upper right next to the heading. This step moves the graphic to the new location. Release the mouse button. Now you can resize the graphic.

3 Move the mouse pointer to the bottom middle selection handle and when the mouse pointer changes to a double-headed arrow, drag the graphic up about one-half inch. This step shrinks the height of the graphic.

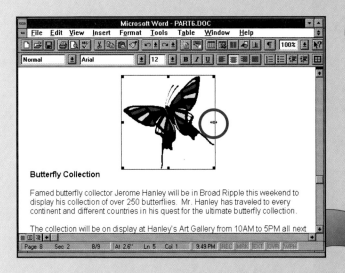

4 Move the mouse pointer to the right middle selection handle and when the mouse pointer changes to a double-headed arrow, drag the graphic to the left about one-half inch. This step makes the graphic narrower.

5 Click outside the graphic. This step deselects the graphic.

WHY WORRY?

Follow the same procedures to move the graphic back to its original location or to change the graphic back to its original size.

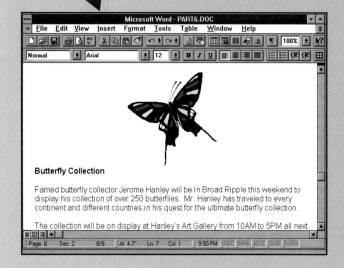

TASK 54
Deleting a Graphic

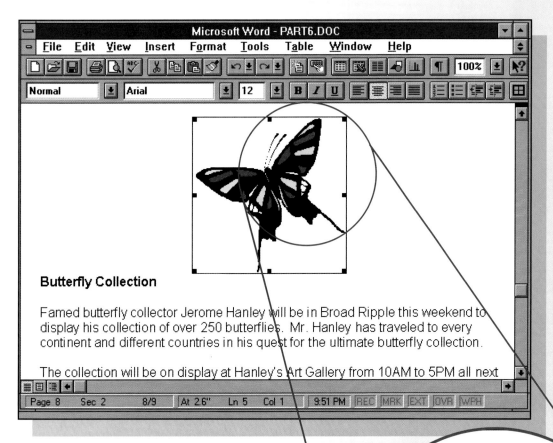

"Why would I do this?"

Once you've inserted a graphic in your document, you may need to delete it.

Let's delete the graphic.

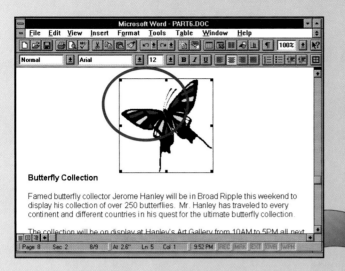

1 Click the graphic. This step selects the graphic that you want to delete. Selection handles appear around the sides of the graphic.

2 Press **Delete**. The graphic is deleted.

WHY WORRY?

To undo the deletion, immediately click the Undo button on the Standard toolbar.

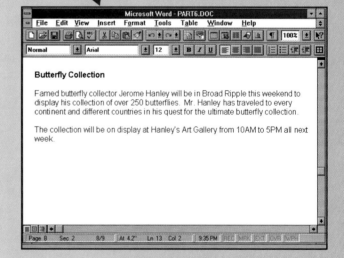

TASK 55
Creating a Table

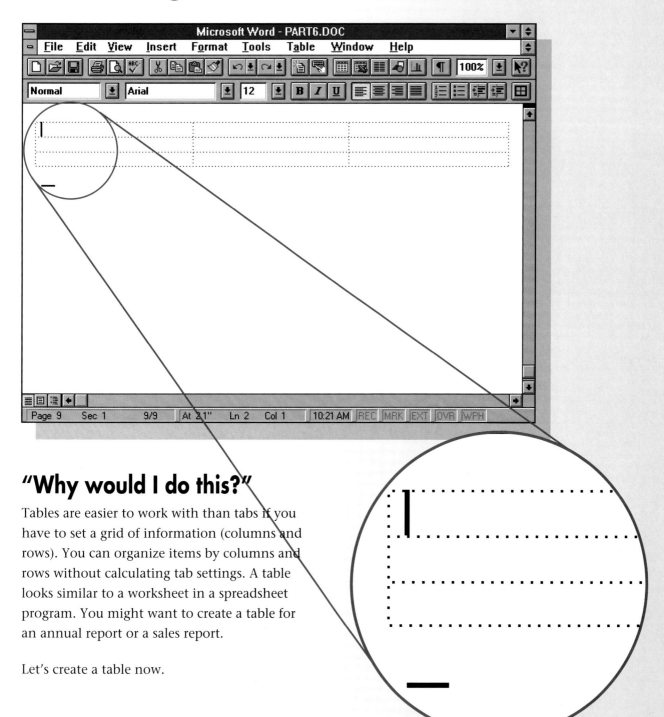

"Why would I do this?"

Tables are easier to work with than tabs if you have to set a grid of information (columns and rows). You can organize items by columns and rows without calculating tab settings. A table looks similar to a worksheet in a spreadsheet program. You might want to create a table for an annual report or a sales report.

Let's create a table now.

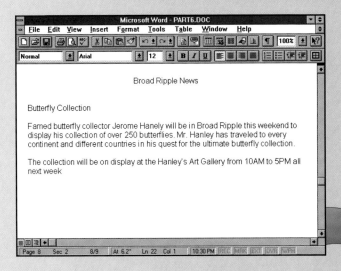

1 Press **Ctrl+End**. This step moves the insertion point to the bottom of the document.

2 Press **Ctrl+Enter**. Then, scroll down so that only page 9 shows on-screen. This step inserts a page break and reorients the screen.

3 Move the mouse pointer to the **Insert Table** button (the button with a piece of paper and three columns) on the Standard toolbar. This step moves the mouse pointer to the button you want to select.

Task 55: Creating a Table

4 Click and hold down the mouse button and drag over the grid to highlight three columns and three rows. You see *3 x 3 Table* at the bottom of the grid. This step tells Word for Windows to create a three-column table with three rows.

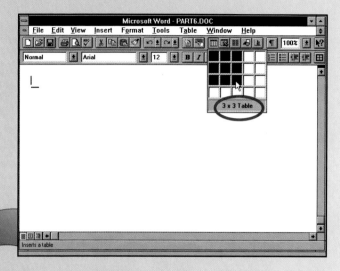

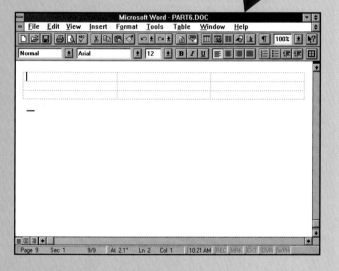

5 Release the mouse button. This step confirms the table and inserts a table with three columns and three rows on-screen.

Entering Text in a Table

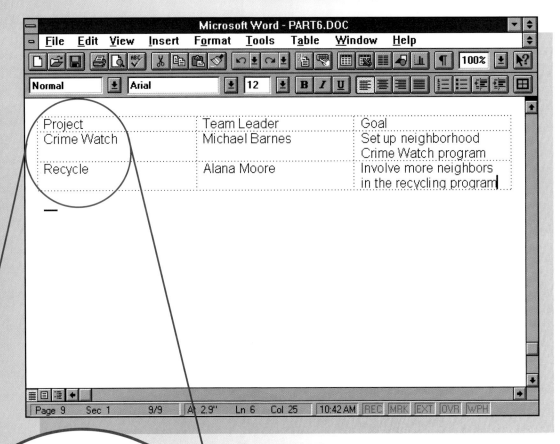

"Why would I do this?"

A Word table contains columns and rows and looks similar to a spreadsheet. The intersection of a row and a column in the table is called a cell. You can enter text in these cells in the table by typing and pressing Tab to move to the next cell.

Let's enter text in your table now.

Task 56: Entering Text in a Table

1 Type **Project** and press **Tab**. This step enters information into the first cell in the table and moves the insertion point to the next column in that row.

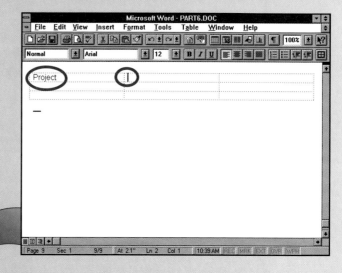

2 Type **Team Leader** and press **Tab**. This step enters information in that cell and moves the insertion point to the next column.

3 Type **Goal** and press **Tab**. This step completes the headings for the table and moves the insertion point to the first cell in the next row.

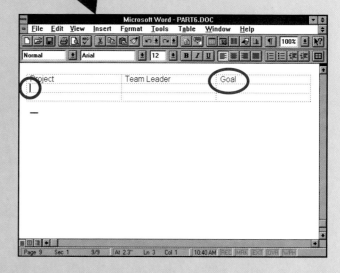

4 Type **Crime Watch** and press **Tab**. Type **Michael Barnes** and press **Tab**. Type **Set up neighborhood Crime Watch program** and press **Tab**. This step enters the text for the first row and moves the insertion point to the next row.

5 Type **Recycle** and press **Tab**. Type **Alana Moore** and press **Tab**. Type **Involve more neighbors in the recycling program**. This step completes the text for the table.

NOTE ▼

Pressing Shift+Tab will move back to the previous cell.

WHY WORRY?

Make corrections in the table as you would in a normal document. You can press Enter within a table cell to insert a line break.

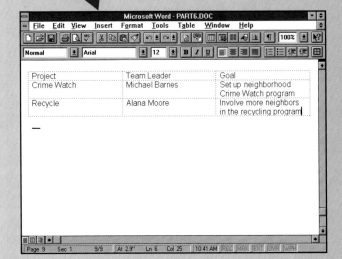

Adding a Row to a Table

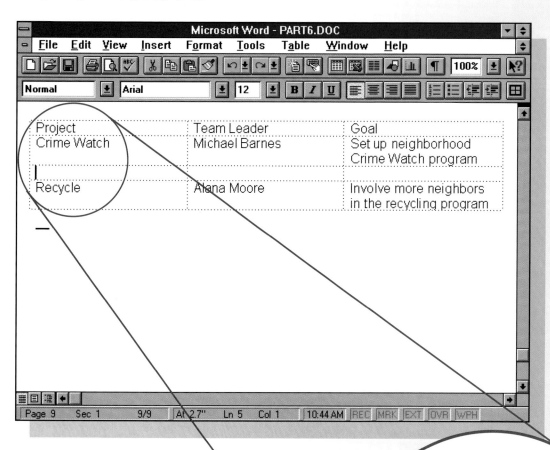

"Why would I do this?"

You can insert a row or column in a table for adding additional text or spacing. In the following task, we will be adding a row to insert text.

Let's add a row to the end of your table now.

1 Put the insertion point where you want to insert a row. To access the Table commands, you have to put the insertion point within the table.

2 Click **Table** in the menu bar. Then, click **Insert Rows**. This step selects the Table Insert Rows command. A row is inserted in the table.

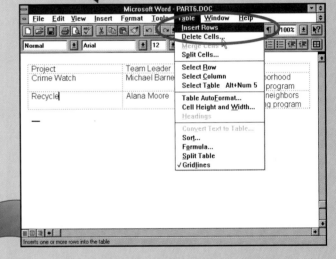

> **NOTE** ▼
>
> As a shortcut, you can put the insertion point in the cell of the last row and column of the table and press Tab to create a new row.

3 Click in the first cell of the new row. Then, type **Membership Drive** and press **Tab**. Type **Barbara Diego** and press **Tab**. Type **Organize membership drive**. This step enters the text for the new row.

> **WHY WORRY?**
>
> To undo the change, click the Undo button on the Standard toolbar. Or delete the row.

Deleting a Row from a Table

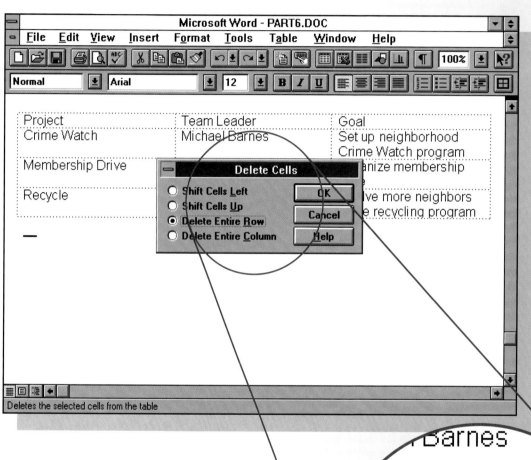

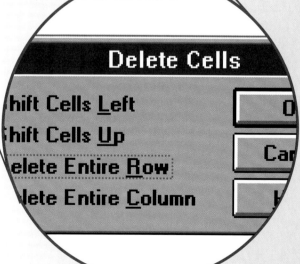

"Why would I do this?"

You might want to delete a row or rows that you no longer want from a table or you may want to close up some empty space.

Let's delete a row from your table now.

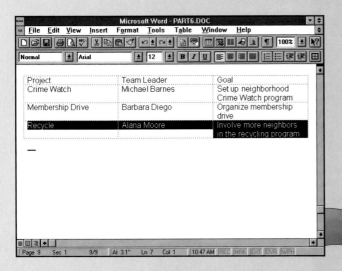

1 Put the insertion point in the last row of the table. To select the row, drag across the entire row.

2 Click **Table** on the menu bar. This step opens the Table menu and displays a list of Table commands.

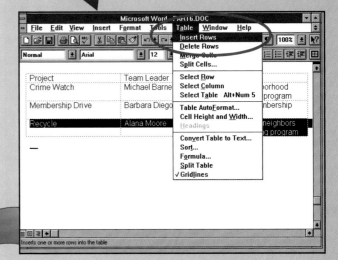

3 Click **Delete Cells**. This step selects the Delete Cells command. You see the Delete Cells dialog box.

4 Click the **Delete Entire Row** option button. This option tells Word for Windows to delete the entire row.

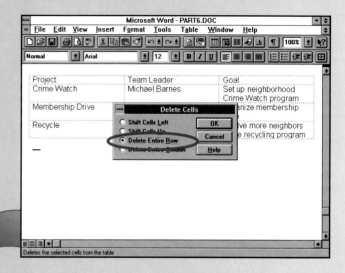

5 Click **OK**. The row is deleted.

WHY WORRY?

To undo the change, click the Undo button on the Standard toolbar.

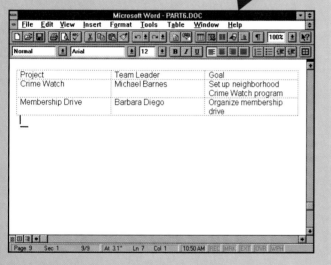

Creating a Two-Column Document

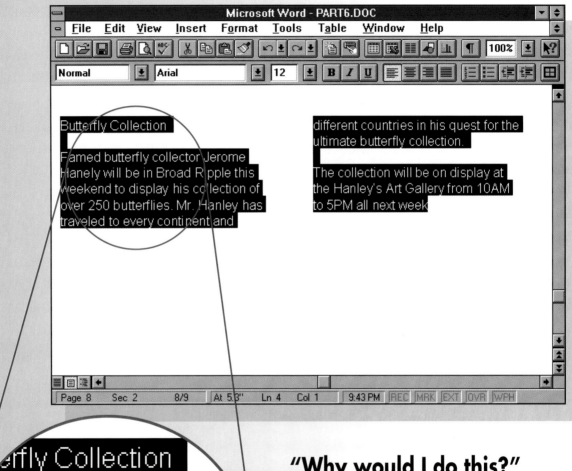

"Why would I do this?"

You can create a two-column document where text flows from one column to the next until all the text is used. Two-column documents work well for newsletters. You can also use columns to create parallel columns, newspaper and magazine columns, or uneven columns for desktop publishing effects.

Let's create two columns using the text from Task 52.

Task 59: Creating a Two-Column Document

1 Move the insertion point to page 8. Select all the text except for the centered title. This step tells Word for Windows where you want to create the columns.

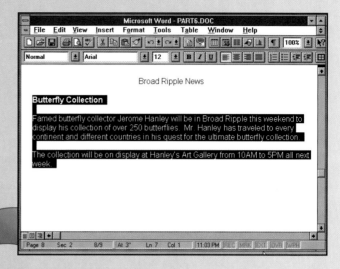

2 Move the mouse pointer to the **Columns** button (the button with two columns) on the Standard toolbar. This step moves the mouse pointer to the button you want to select.

3 Click and hold down the mouse button and drag over the columns to highlight two columns. You see *2 Columns* at the bottom of the columns. This step tells Word for Windows to create two columns.

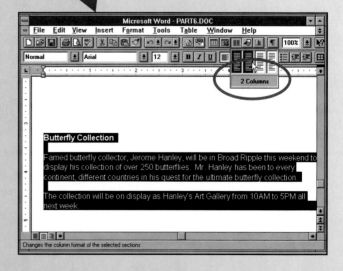

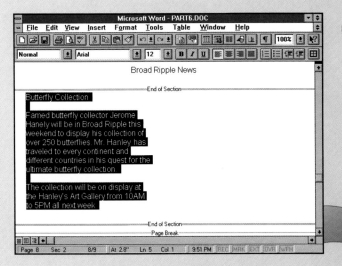

4 Release the mouse button. On-screen, you cannot see the two columns. To do so, you must switch to Page Layout view.

5 Click the **Page Layout View** button (the button with a piece of paper and three short lines) on the status bar. You now have a two-column page. The current text is reformatted into two columns.

WHY WORRY?

To undo the columns, click the Undo button on the Standard toolbar immediately.

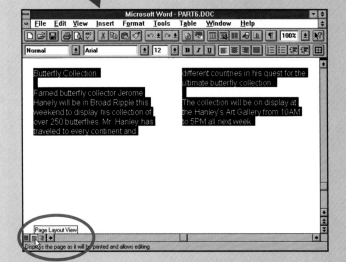

Inserting a WordArt Object

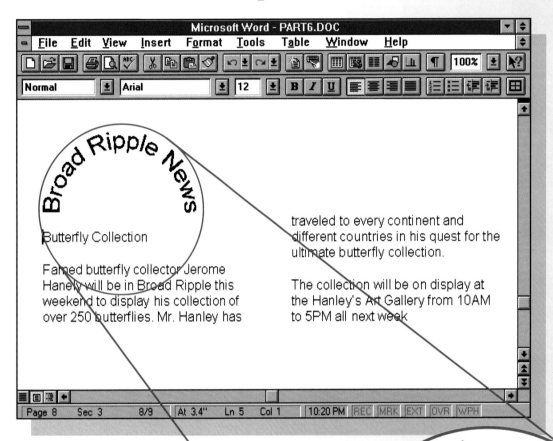

"Why would I do this?"

You can create a special text effect with Microsoft WordArt 2.0. This feature enables you to give plain text design and shapes. For example, you can use any TrueType font and arch the text. WordArt is useful for creating desktop publishing effects.

Let's arch the words *Broad Ripple News*.

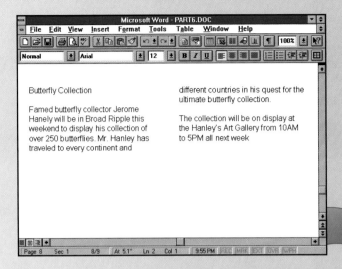

1 Click above **Butterfly Collection**. This step moves the insertion point to where you want to insert the object.

NOTE ▼

The document should already be in Page Layout view from the previous task. If not, click the Page Layout View button (the button with a piece of paper and three short lines) on the status bar. This step switches the document to Page Layout view.

2 Click **Insert** on the menu bar. Then, click **Object**. This step selects the Insert Object command. You see the Object dialog box. The Create New tab is selected.

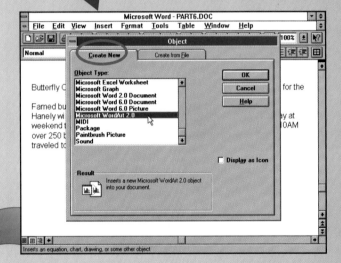

3 Double-click **Microsoft WordArt 2.0**. This step tells Word for Windows that you want to insert a WordArt object. You may have to scroll through the list to find this option. You see the Enter Your Text Here dialog box.

Task 60: Inserting a WordArt Object

4 Type **Broad Ripple News**. This step enters the text you want.

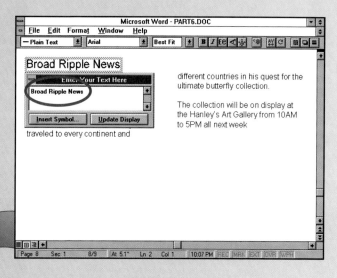

5 Click the down arrow next to the Plain Text option on the WordArt Toolbar. Then, click the arch in the second row, first column. This step tells Word for Windows that you want to arch the text.

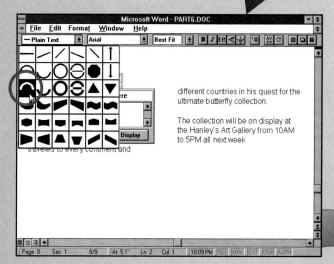

6 Click back in the document. Then, click outside the selected object so that you can see the object better. This step inserts the object in the document and returns you to the document.

WHY WORRY?

To edit the object, double-click it. To delete the object, click it once and press Delete.

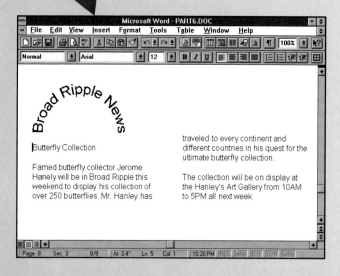

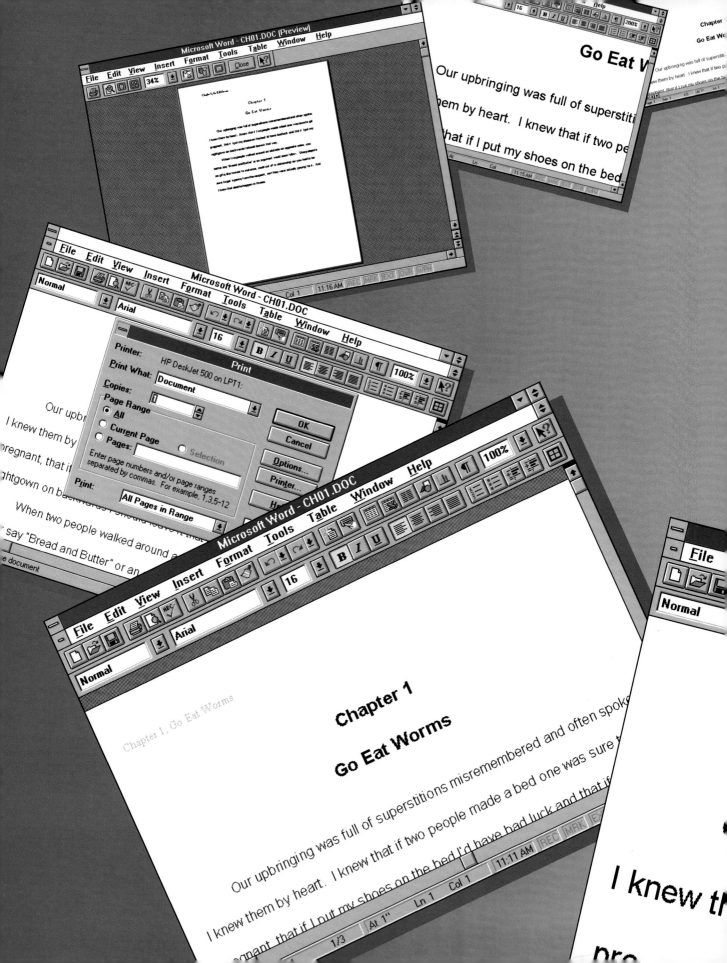

PART VII

Viewing and Printing the Document

61 Displaying a Document in Page Layout View

62 Zooming a Document

63 Previewing the Document

64 Printing the Document

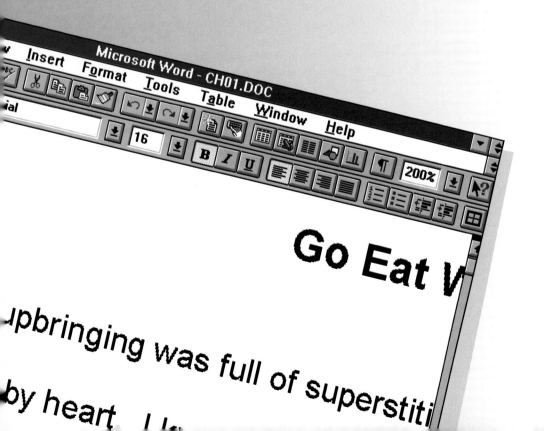

Part VII: Viewing and Printing the Document

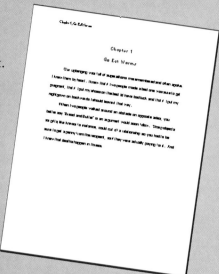

In this part, you learn how to change the view of your document, preview your document, and then print your document.

The Page Layout view enables you to display multiple columns, headers and footers, and footnotes in the document.

Word's Zoom feature lets you enlarge or reduce the view of a page on-screen. Text on the screen can be smaller or larger, and may show the whole page or a smaller section of it at higher magnification.

With Word's Print Preview feature, you can review the appearance of the printed document before you produce the final output. The first page of the document appears as a reduced image in the Print Preview screen. However, you can use the Zoom feature in Print Preview to magnify the view. This allows you to inspect the printout more closely. Then, when you click the Zoom button again, Word reduces the view to a smaller image again. You can also shrink the document to fit on one page and start printing from the Preview window. See your Microsoft Word documentation for complete information.

In Word, you can print your documents using a basic printing procedure, or you can enhance the printout using several page setup options as explained earlier in Part V. It is fairly simple to print a document in Word.

The first time you use your printer with Word, it is a good idea to check the Setup options. Word can use the options and capabilities that are available with each printer. Often, you will need to provide more details about your printer so that Word knows the capabilities available. If you want to specify details about your printer, choose the File Print command and click the Printer button. Then you can confirm that you installed the right printer and connected it correctly, or you can switch to a different printer.

It is a good idea to save your documents before printing—just in case a printer error or other problem occurs. You won't lose any work since the last time you saved the document. You learn how to print your document from the Print dialog box. But if you already set up your print options and you're back to the document, you can just click the Print button on the Standard toolbar to print your document.

In Word, the Print dialog box lets you print some or all of the pages within a document, the current page, a range of pages, selected text, or multiple copies of the printout.

This part introduces you to the basics of printing the document. With some experimentation and practice, you will be able to create some very interesting printed results.

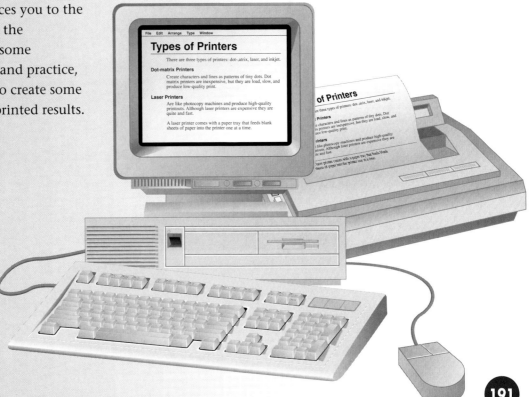

Displaying a Document in Page Layout View

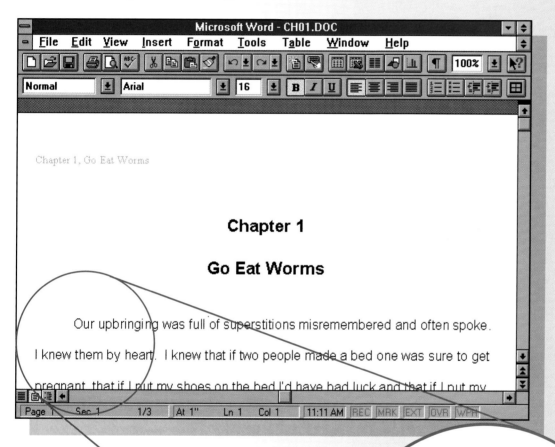

"Why would I do this?"

Page Layout view lets you view your document as it will be printed, while retaining all editing features and capabilities (unlike Print Preview). In Page Layout view, you see headers, footers, multiple columns, and footnotes in your document. This feature is useful when you make formatting changes and need to see the results.

Display your CH01.DOC document in Page Layout view.

Task 61: Displaying a Document in Page Layout View

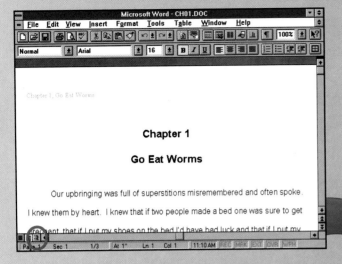

1 Click the **Page Layout View** button. Clicking the Page Layout View button selects the View Page Layout command. You see the document in Page Layout view. As you can see, the header appears in this view.

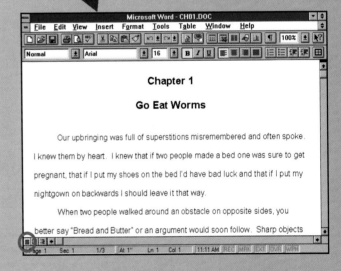

2 Click the **Normal View** button at the beginning of the Status bar (the button with several horizontal lines). This step returns the document to normal view.

WHY WORRY?

The Page Layout command is not a toggle. To turn off Page Layout view, you must select another view. To return to Normal view, click the Normal View button on the Status bar.

Zooming a Document

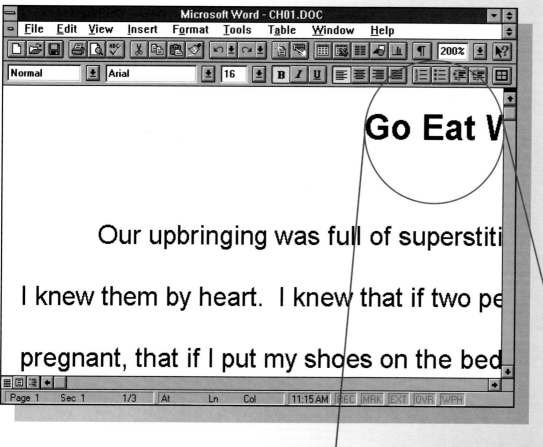

"Why would I do this?"

If you want to zoom in and get a closer look at text in your document, select a higher percentage of magnification. For instance, if you work with small font sizes, you can inspect this closely without having to preview or print the document. If you want to zoom out so the whole page shows on the screen at one glance, select a lower percentage of magnification.

Let's examine how to zoom in on your document, and then zoom out. Last, you will return to the 100% view.

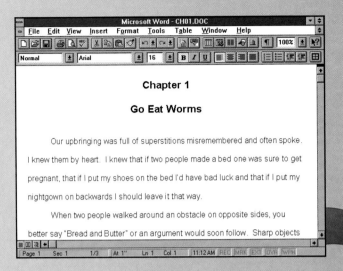

1 Press **Ctrl+Home** to reorient the screen.

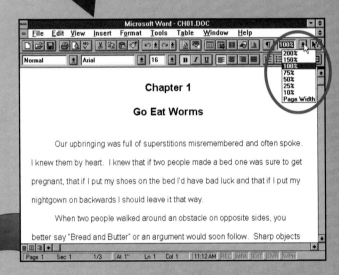

2 Click the **down arrow** next to the Zoom Control box on the Standard toolbar.

3 Now click **200%**. This step enlarges the document to a magnification of 200%.

Task 62: Zooming a Document

4 Click the **down arrow** next to the Zoom Control box again. Then click **50%**. This step reduces the document to 50%.

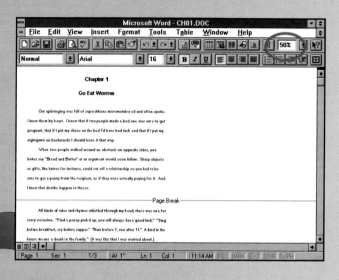

5 Click **100%** in the Zoom Control box to restore the document to 100%.

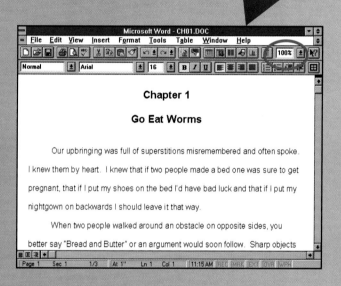

WHY WORRY?

If you select the wrong magnification percentage, just switch to the percentage you want.

TASK 63

Previewing the Document

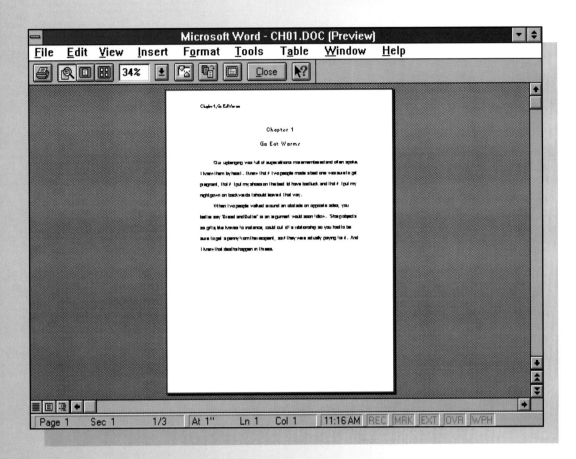

"Why would I do this?"

Print Preview lets you see document pages on-screen as they will appear printed on paper, including page numbers, headers, footers, fonts, font sizes and styles, orientation, and margins. Previewing your document is a great way to catch formatting errors, such as incorrect margins, overlapped text, boldfaced text, and other text enhancements. You will save costly printer paper and time by first previewing your document.

Let's preview your document now.

Task 63: Previewing the Document

1 Click the **Print Preview** button on the Standard toolbar. Clicking the Print Preview button selects the Print Preview command. You see a preview of how your document will look when you print it.

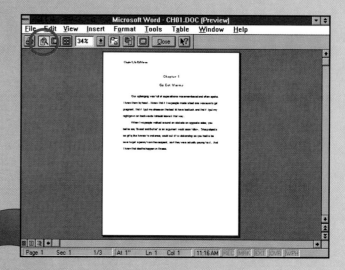

NOTE ▼

To preview the document, your monitor must have graphics capability. Try this procedure. If you see an error message, your monitor probably cannot display the document. You must print the document to see how it looks.

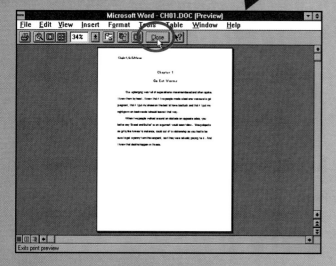

2 To exit Print Preview, click the **Close** button. This step returns you to the document.

NOTE ▼

You can also press the Esc key to quit Print Preview.

WHY WORRY?

To exit Print Preview, click on the Close button.

Printing the Document

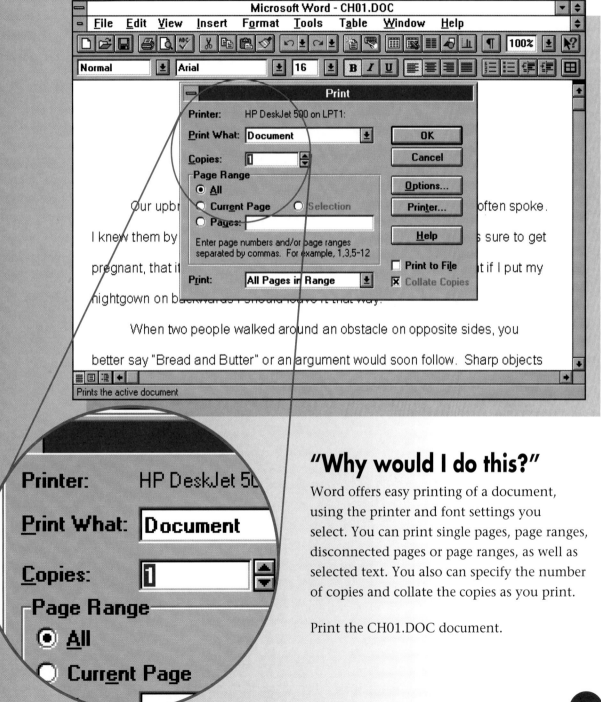

"Why would I do this?"

Word offers easy printing of a document, using the printer and font settings you select. You can print single pages, page ranges, disconnected pages or page ranges, as well as selected text. You also can specify the number of copies and collate the copies as you print.

Print the CH01.DOC document.

Task 64: Printing the Document

1 Click **File** on the menu bar. Then, click **Print**. This step selects the File Print command. Word opens the Print dialog box. You see the name of your printer at the top of the dialog box. This dialog box enables you to control what you print (the entire document, a range of pages, and so on), how many copies you print, and other options.

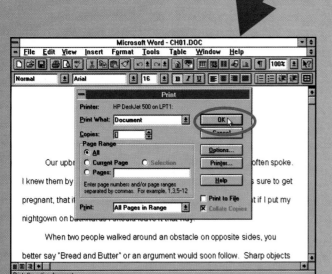

2 Click **OK** to start printing the document.

NOTE ▼

When you installed the Word program, you also installed the printer. If no printer is installed, refer to the Word manual.

WHY WORRY?

While the document is printing, Word displays a dialog box on-screen. To stop the print job, click Cancel.

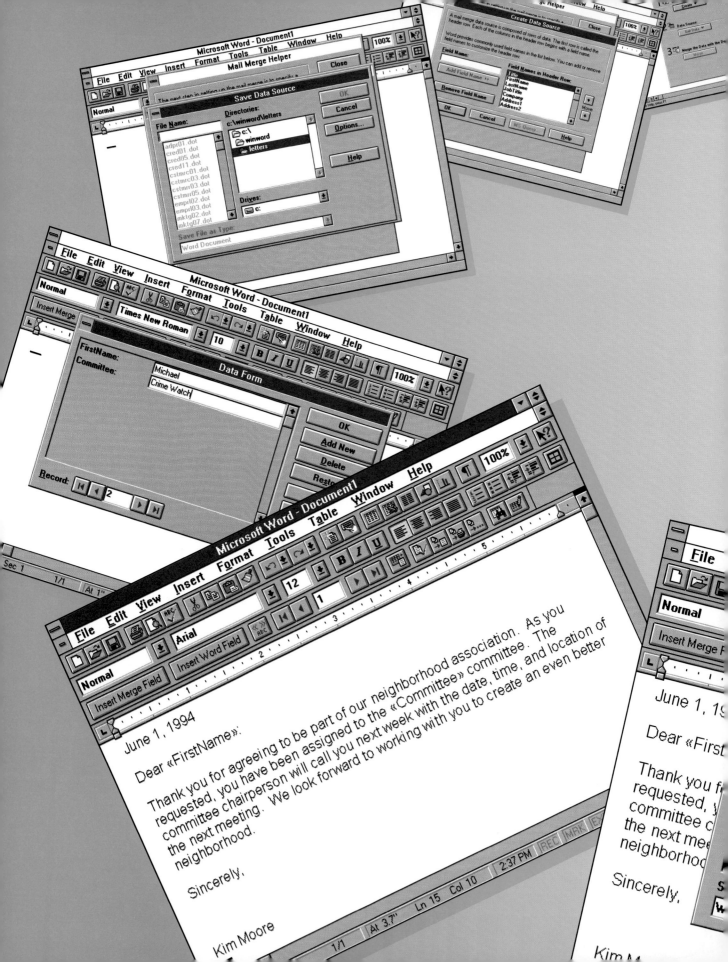

PART VIII

Merging

65 Creating a Main Document

66 Creating a Data Source

67 Saving the Data Source

68 Entering Records into the Data Source

69 Typing the Main Document

70 Saving the Main Document

71 Merging the Files

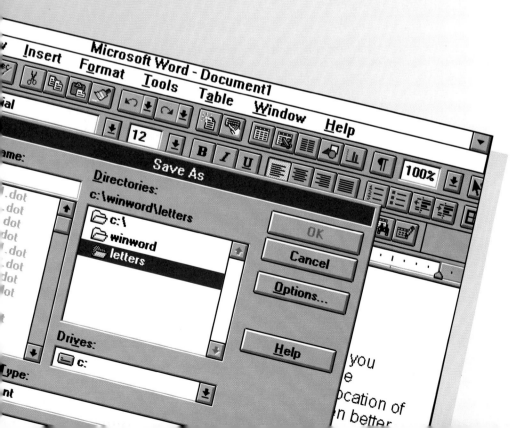

In this part, you learn how to create a merge letter, which is an involved process. The tasks in this part all build on each other and follow one right after the other. You should follow all the tasks in the section to complete the merge process.

Two files make up a basic merge procedure: the data source and the main document. The main document contains the unchanging text and the codes that control the merge. The data source contains the field definition and the variable information you want inserted into the main document.

Butterfly Collection

Famed butterfly collector, Jerome Hanley, will be in Broad Ripple this weekend to display his collection of over 250 butterflies. Mr. Hanley has been to every continent, 50 different countries in his quest for the ultimate butterfly collection.

The collection will be on display in Hanley's Art Gallery from 10AM to 5PM all next week.

There are several tasks you must follow to create a merge letter. First you create the main document. Next you create the data source. Word provides several predefined fields that you can use in the data source, or you can create your own.

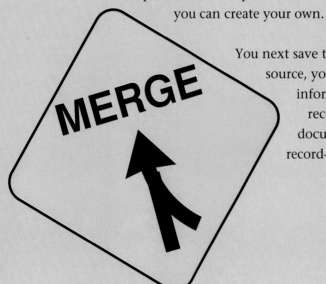

You next save the data source. After you save the data source, you enter records. A record is one set of information. Each individual element in the record is stored in a field. You will create a document—with the specific information in that record—for each record you enter.

Next you type the main document. The main document contains the text of the letter—the information you want each letter to contain. The main document also includes the codes that control the merge. You need to know the names of the fields you create in the data source so that you can insert the right code into the main document.

After you create the main document, you save the file. The final step is to merge the two files. A new file will be created that contains a letter for each record in the data source. You can save the new file or just print it.

Word's Mail Merge feature offers many options; it can be a pretty complex feature. This book covers the simplest example. If you want more information, see your Microsoft Word documentation.

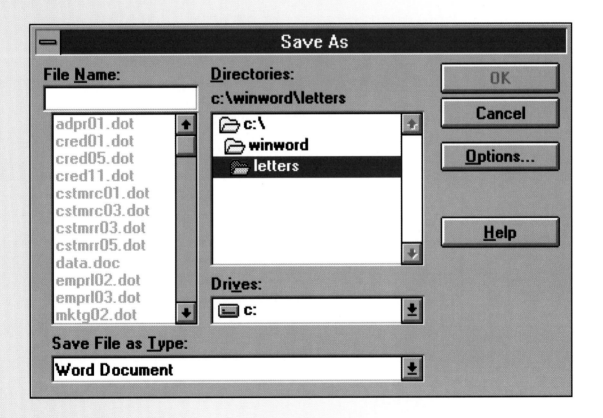

Creating a Main Document

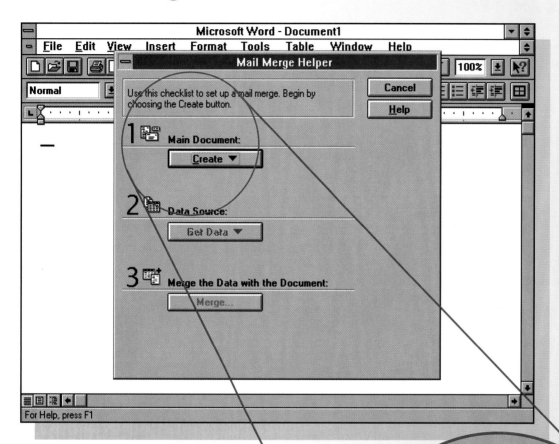

"Why would I do this?"

Before you can merge files, you must create a main document file. The main document file contains field names and the information that remains constant. Each field name corresponds to a field name in the data file. You might want to create a main document that contains an invitation, a product announcement, or a price list.

Let's create a main document now. Later you will type the text in the main document after you define the data source.

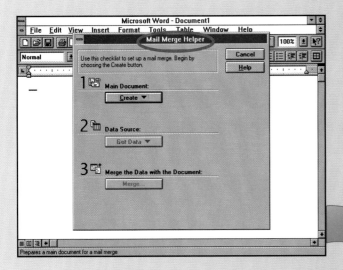

1 Click **Tools** on the menu bar. Then click **Mail Merge**. Word opens the Merge Mail Helper dialog box. You first select the type of file that you want to create.

2 Click **Create** to display a drop-down list of options. Here you select the type of main document you are creating. Click **Form Letters**. This step tells Word that you are creating a form letter. You are prompted whether you want to open a new document or create the document within the active window.

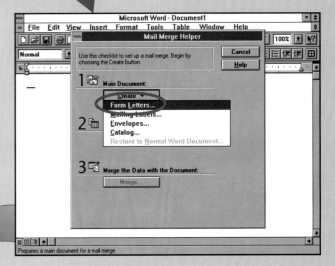

3 Click **Active Window**. This step tells Word that you will use the active window to create the main document. You are returned to the Mail Merge Helper dialog box. Next you create the data source.

WHY WORRY?

If you don't want to create the main document, click Cancel.

Creating a Data Source

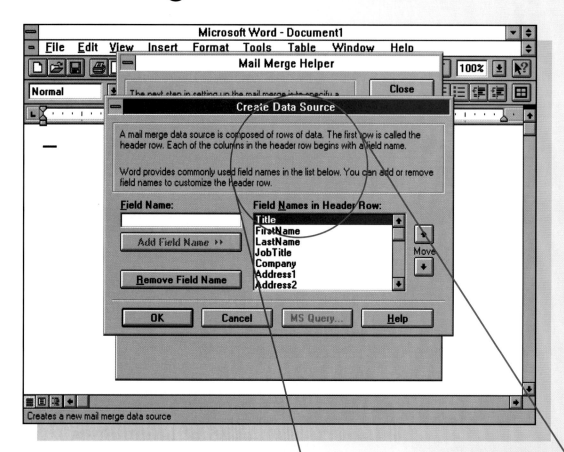

"Why would I do this?"

The data source stores the variable information that you want to insert into the form field. Each piece of information is stored in a field; a set of information is called a record. Perhaps you want to create a data source file of addresses for batch mailing.

Let's create a data source file. Then, in the next task, you save the data source file. After you save the file, you enter the records.

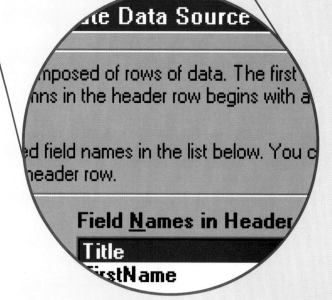

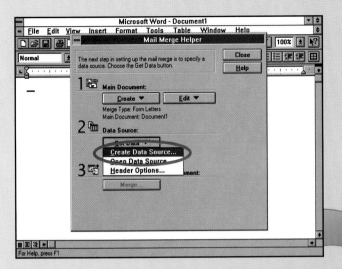

1 From the Mail Merge Helper dialog box, click **Get Data**. Word displays a drop-down list of data source options.

2 Click **Create Data Source**. This step tells Word that you want to create the data source. You see the Create Data Source dialog box. This box includes a field name list with common field names. You will use one of these fields, **FirstName**, and then add a new field name.

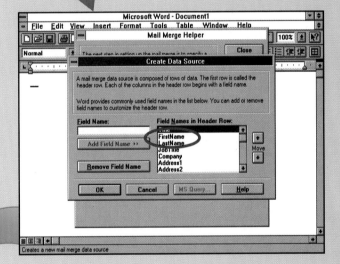

3 Type **Committee**. This step enters a new field name in the Field Name text box.

Task 66: Creating a Data Source

4 Click **Add Field Name**. This step adds this field to the list for your data source.

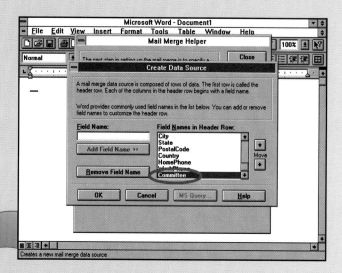

5 In the Field Names in Header Row list, scroll to the top of the list and click **Title**. This step selects a field you don't need.

6 Click **Remove Field Name**. This step removes the field.

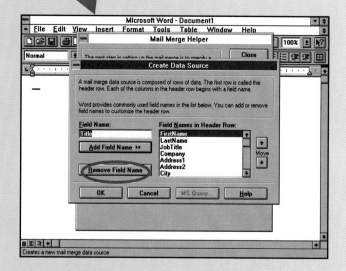

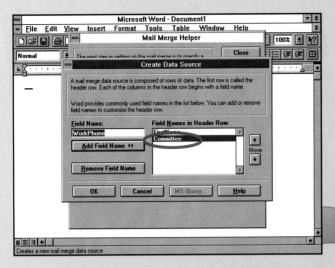

7 Follow steps 5 and 6 to remove the **LastName**, **JobTitle**, **Company**, **Address1**, **Address2**, **City**, **State**, **PostalCode**, **Country**, **HomePhone**, and **WorkPhone** fields. This step removes some of the predefined fields.

8 Click **OK**. This step completes the field name list. The Save Data Source dialog box is displayed so that you can save the field. See the next task.

WHY WORRY?

If you don't want to create the data source, click Cancel.

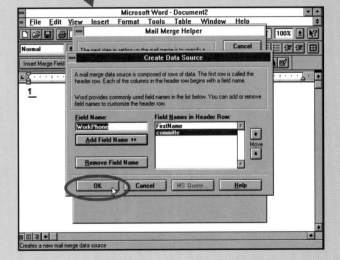

Saving the Data Source

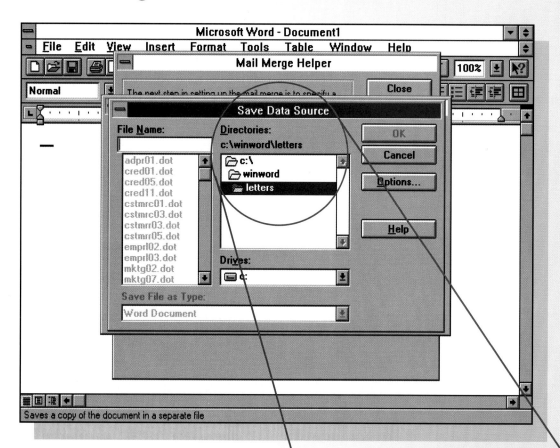

"Why would I do this?"

After you create the data source file, you must save the file. Then you can add records to the data source file. As you add records, you should periodically save the file. Select File Save or press Ctrl+S to save the file.

Let's save our data source file now.

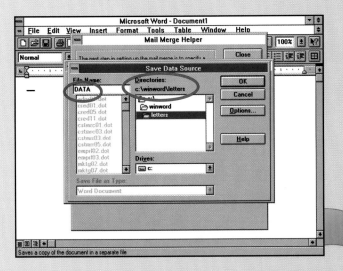

1 After you enter the field names, type **DATA** in the File Name text box of the Save Data Source dialog box. The current directory is C:\WINWORD\LETTERS. That is where the file will be saved. This step enters the name for the data source.

2 Click **OK**. This step saves the document. You are reminded that no records have been created.

WHY WORRY?

If you don't want to save the file, click Cancel.

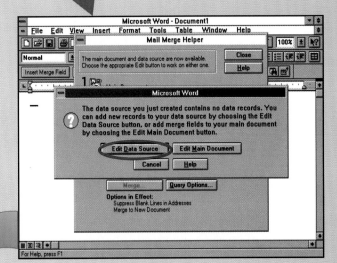

3 Click **Edit Data Source**. This step tells Word that you will add the records. You see the Data Form dialog box appear. Proceed to the next task to complete this box.

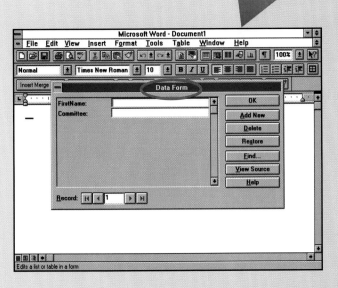

Entering Records into the Data Source

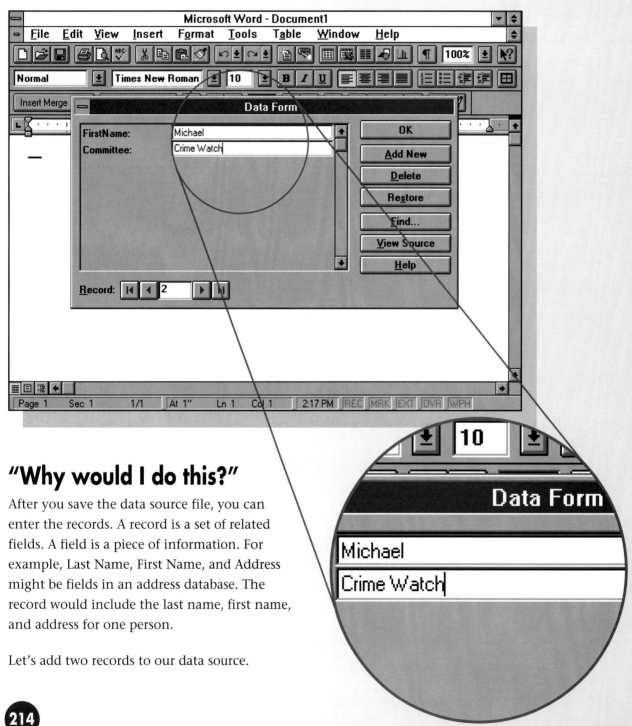

"Why would I do this?"

After you save the data source file, you can enter the records. A record is a set of related fields. A field is a piece of information. For example, Last Name, First Name, and Address might be fields in an address database. The record would include the last name, first name, and address for one person.

Let's add two records to our data source.

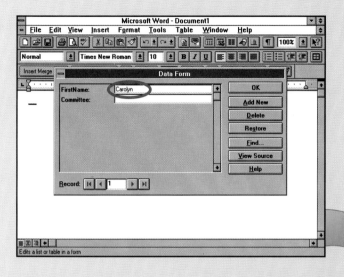

1 After you save the data source, type **Carolyn** in the First Name text box of the Data Form dialog box. This step enters the information for the first field. When you merge the documents, this specific text will be inserted into the document.

2 Press **Tab** to move the insertion point to the Committee text box. Then type **Recycle**. This step enters the specific committee for this person. This information (the name and committee) is stored in a record.

WHY WORRY?

If you make a mistake while typing, correct it as you would in any other document.

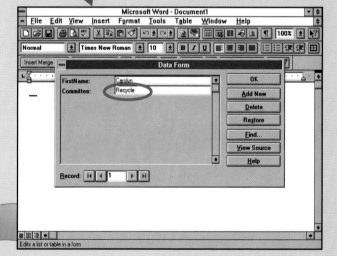

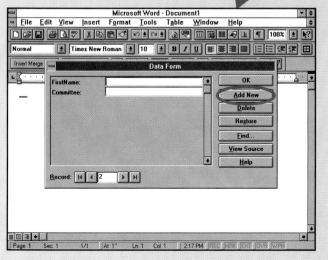

3 Click **Add New**. This step selects the Add New button. The current record is added to the document. The text boxes are cleared and the record count is incremented by one, so the next record can be entered.

4 Type **Michael**. This step enters the information in the first field of the second record.

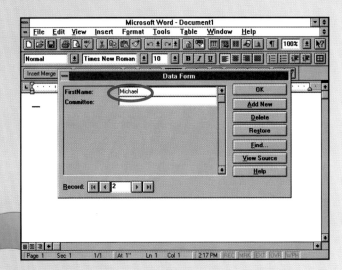

5 Press **Tab** to move the insertion point to the next field. Then type **Crime Watch**. This step enters the information for the next field.

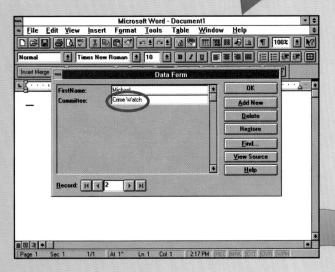

6 Click **OK**. This step selects the OK button and adds the record to the data document. You are returned to the main document. The Mail Merge toolbar is displayed. In the next task, you will type the main document.

NOTE ▼

To delete a record, use the Record scroll arrows at the bottom of the Data Form to display the record you want. Then click the Delete button.

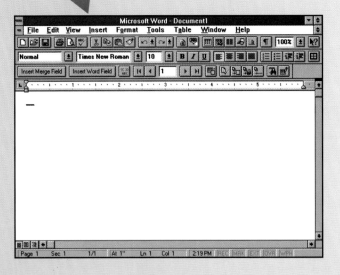

Typing the
Main Document

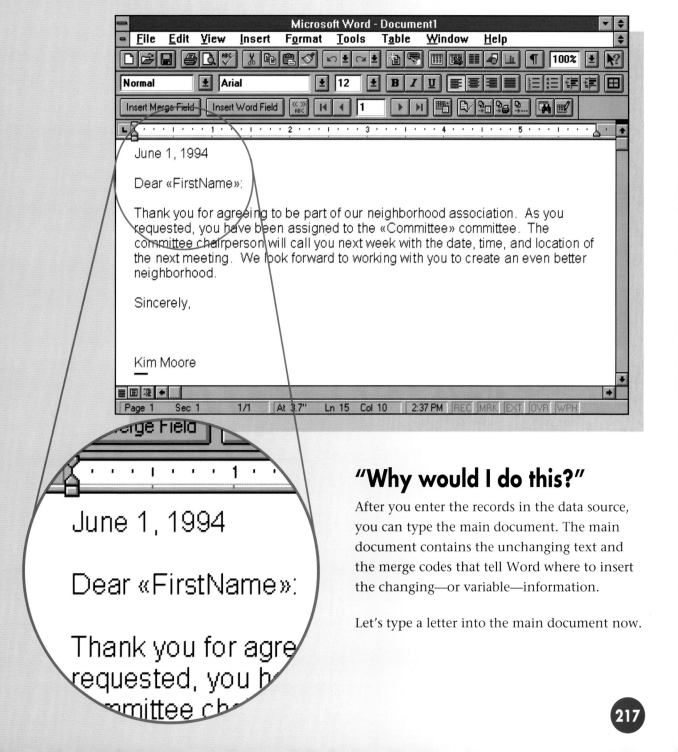

"Why would I do this?"

After you enter the records in the data source, you can type the main document. The main document contains the unchanging text and the merge codes that tell Word where to insert the changing—or variable—information.

Let's type a letter into the main document now.

1 Type **June 1, 1994** and press **Enter** twice. Type **Dear** and press the **space bar**. This step enters the beginning text for the main document. Now you are ready to insert a field.

WHY WORRY?

If you make a mistake while typing, correct it as you would in any regular document.

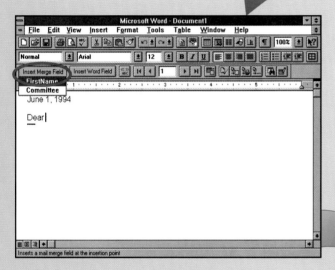

2 Click **Insert Merge Field**. This step selects the Insert Merge Field button and displays a drop-down list of field names.

3 Click **First Name**. This step inserts the field name. You see the field code on-screen. This code tells Word to insert the information into the first field of each record.

WHY WORRY?

If you insert the field incorrectly, select it and press the Delete key. Then try again.

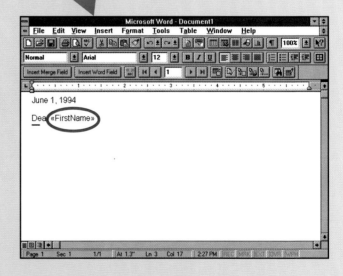

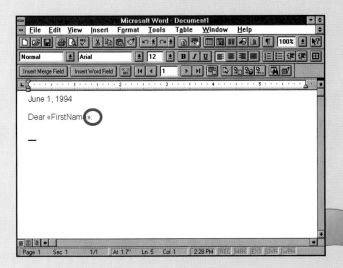

4 Type **:** and press **Enter** twice. This step finishes the greeting for the letter.

5 Type the middle of the letter: **Thank you for agreeing to be part of our neighborhood association. As you requested, you have been assigned to the**. This step enters more of the unchanging text. Be sure to press the **space bar** after *the*. You are now ready to insert the next field.

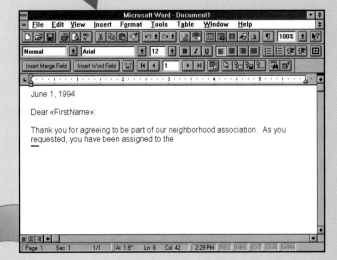

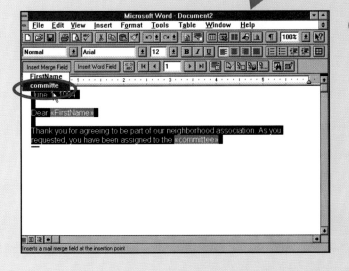

6 Click **Insert Merge Field**. This step selects the Insert Merge Field button and displays a drop-down list of field names.

Task 69: Typing the Main Document

7 Click **Committee**. This step inserts the field code into your document. You will see the field code on-screen. This code tells Word to insert the information into the first field of each record.

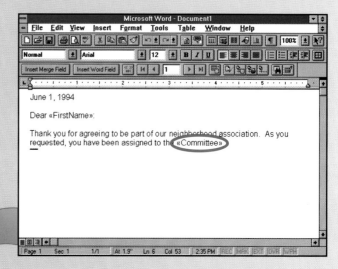

8 Type the rest of the letter: **committee. The committee chairperson will call you next week with the date, time, and location of the next meeting. We look forward to working with you to create an even better neighborhood.**

Sincerely,

Kim Moore

This step completes the letter. To save this completed letter, perform the steps as described in the next task.

Saving the Main Document

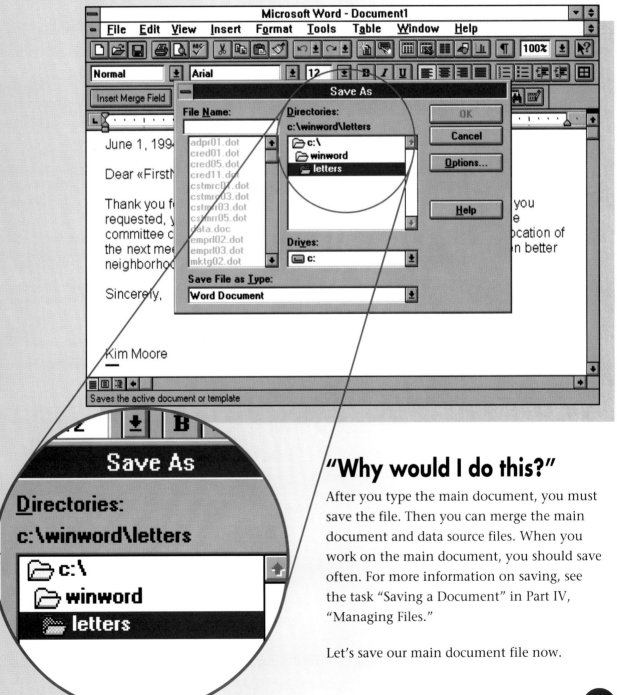

"Why would I do this?"

After you type the main document, you must save the file. Then you can merge the main document and data source files. When you work on the main document, you should save often. For more information on saving, see the task "Saving a Document" in Part IV, "Managing Files."

Let's save our main document file now.

Task 70: Saving the Main Document

1 Click **File** on the menu bar. Then, click **Save As**. This step selects the File Save As command. You see the Save As dialog box.

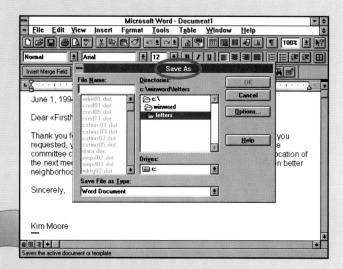

2 Type **MAIN**. This step enters the name for the main document. The current directory is C:\WINWORD\LETTERS. That is where the file will be saved.

WHY WORRY?

If you don't want to save the file, click Cancel.

3 Click **OK**. This step saves the document. The document remains open on-screen and the file name appears on the title bar.

Merging the Files

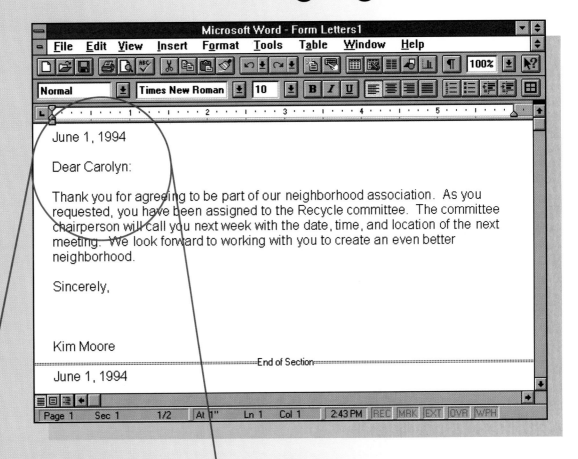

June 1, 1994

Dear Carolyn:

Thank you for agreeing to be part of our neighborhood association. As you requested, you have been assigned to the Recycle committee. The committee chairperson will call you next week with the date, time, and location of the next meeting. We look forward to working with you to create an even better neighborhood.

Sincerely,

Kim Moore

"Why would I do this?"

The last step in the merge process is to merge the main document file and the data source file. Word will create a new file that contains a letter for each record in the data source. You can save the new file or just print it. The Mail Merge feature offers many options that enable you to control how a merge is performed. If you want more information, see your Microsoft Word documentation.

Let's merge our two files now.

Task 71: Merging the Files

1 Click the **Mail Merge Helper** button. This step selects the Tools Mail Merge command. You see the Mail Merge Helper dialog box.

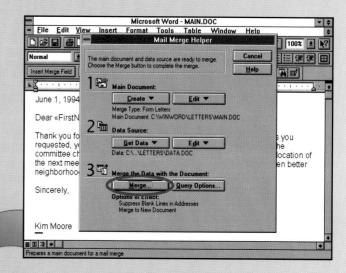

2 Click **Merge**. This step selects the Merge button. You see the Merge dialog box. Options here enable you to control which records are merged, where the letters are created, and other options. Here the default options are acceptable.

3 Click **Merge**. A specialized letter is created for each record in the data information. The form letter's text is the same. For each field code, information is pulled from the data source. You can merge to the printer or merge all letters into a document with each letter a separate page.

WHY WORRY?

If the merge didn't go as planned, check that you set up each file correctly.

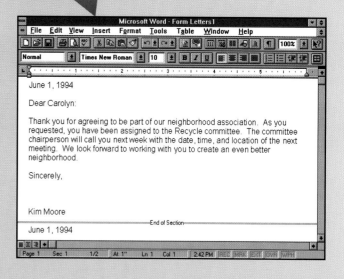

February 18, 1994

Kim Cohen
55 Mountain Road
Rocky Hill, CT 06067

Dear Mrs. Cohen:

Thank you for your recent interest in our astrology programs. Psychic Software offers several types of software to help you get in touch with your psychic nature. Here are some packages that might interest you:

√ Chart your biorhythms with the Rhythm
√ Create astrological charts with Zodiac
√ Do tarot card readings with Tarot Cards
√ Read palms with Palm Reader

I've enclosed a free copy of the Rhythm program for your enjoyment. If you have any questions, please call our 800 number.

Sincerely,

If you are interested in joining the Fitness Health Club, please stop by Human Resources. We have set up a special corporate arrangement so that you can get discounts on memberships for you or your entire family.

TKO Toys
Sales Report

Executive Summary

Sales increased 15% this year.

Five new products were introduced.

Operating costs continued to rise, with a 8% increase this year.

Division Sales

The following table shows a breakdown of sales by division. As you can see, the East and North divisions continued to dominate sales. The fourth quarter increase can be attributed to the introduction of three new products that g...

	1st Quarter	2nd Quarter	3rd Quarter	4th Quarter
East	120,000			
West	80,000	150,000		
North	100,000	90,000	135,000	225,000
South	70,000	125,000	85,000	160,000
		60,000	135,000	20...
			60,000	

New Products

The following new products were releas...

Dinosaur Robots
Queenie Dolls
Little Miss Twinkle Toys
Terror Trolls

Sales Report

Nancy Tumarkin
150 Grapevine Road
Beverly Farms, MA 01916

EDUCATION

Master of Business Administration, Boston University, Boston, Massachusetts.

Bachelor of Science degree in communications, Boston University, Boston, Massachusetts.
Graduated magna cum laude.

EXPERIENCE

Vice President of Marketing, MRO Corporation.
- Manage staff of 30 public relations specialists, copy writers, and product designers.
- Coordinate and plan all marketing pieces: catalogs, promotional pieces, direct mail.
- Responsible for look and design of all company products.
- Responsible for budget of 1.2 million.

Director of New Products, MRO Corporation.
- Design and suggest new product lines.
- Work with product designers and engineers to ensure quality product.
- Coordinate product testing and product launches.
- Developed and launched 3 new product lines during tenure.
- New product lines generated 3.5 million in net revenue.

Advertising Director, S&O Advertising.
- Managed 15 account representatives, ensuring all clients received quality work. Directly worked for the top 2 accounts, designing and coordinating advertising campaigns.
- Solicited new clients.
- Added 7 new clients.

Managing Editor, Boston 128 News
- Manage staff of 20 writers, editors, and page layout.
- Direct editorial staff on selecting articles and feature stories
- Coordinate printing and production process.
- Circulation grew 15% during tenure as managing editor.

REFERENCES

...upon request.

Bu...

Fam...
Hanl...
week...
over 2...
been t...
countrie...
butterfly...

The collection w...
Hanley's Art Gall...
5PM all next week...

New Store Opens

Part IX

Sample Documents

▼ Create a memo

▼ Create a business letter

▼ Create a report

▼ Create a resume

▼ Create a newsletter

▼ Create an invitation

▼ Create a contract

Broad Ripple News

Spring 1994

ction

collector, Jerome
Broad Ripple this
y his collection of
s. Mr. Hanley has
nent, 50 different
st for the ultimate

As a grand opening special, all
merchandise will be 20% off for the
month of March.

Annual Spring Fair

The Broad Ripple Spring Fair is
scheduled for April 4 at the Broad
Ripple Park. Art booths, food, and
entertainment all make the fair the
place to be.

This year over 50 local artists will be
displaying their work. Some artists
will be providing demonstrations and
discussing artistic techniques.

Entertainment will be provided by
the Spinsations, a local band. Also,
clowns, jugglers, and storytellers
will be around to delight the children
attending.

Look for Joe and Ann's BBQ tent.
Other local restaurants will provide
tasty treats and refreshing drinks.

play in
AM to

Part IX: Sample Documents

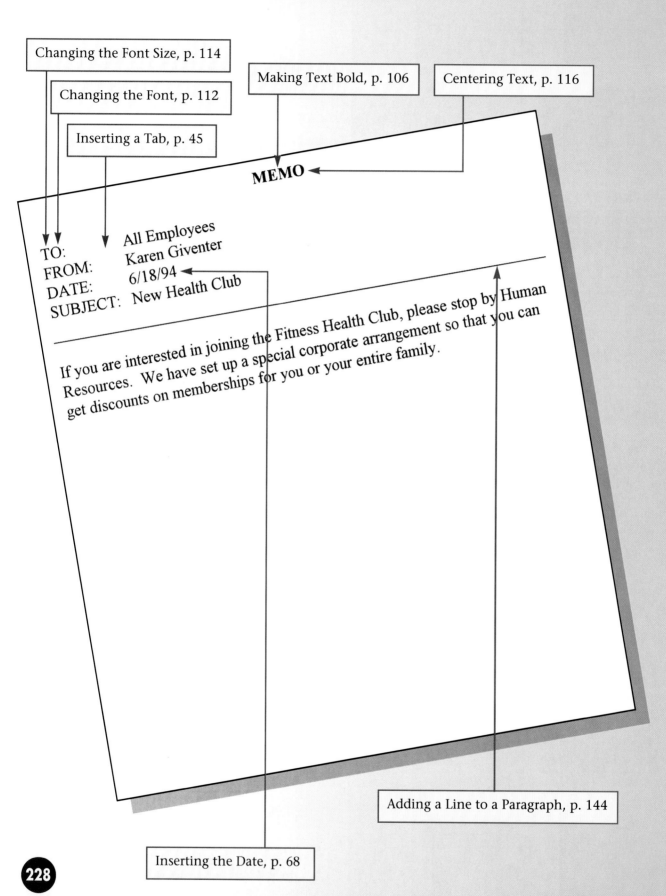

Changing the Font Size, p. 114

Changing the Font, p. 112

Inserting a Tab, p. 45

Making Text Bold, p. 106

Centering Text, p. 116

MEMO

TO: All Employees
FROM: Karen Giventer
DATE: 6/18/94
SUBJECT: New Health Club

If you are interested in joining the Fitness Health Club, please stop by Human Resources. We have set up a special corporate arrangement so that you can get discounts on memberships for you or your entire family.

Adding a Line to a Paragraph, p. 144

Inserting the Date, p. 68

Create a memo

1 Change the font to Times New Roman 14 point. These tasks cover font changes:

Changing the Font   *p. 112*

Changing the Font Size   *p. 114*

2 Type, center, and boldface the heading. See these tasks for help on this step:

Centering Text   *p. 116*

Making Text Bold   *p. 106*

3 Type **TO:**, press **Tab**, and type **All Employees**. Do this for each line of the memo "address." Rather than type the date, you can insert it automatically. See these tasks:

Inserting a Tab   *p. 45*

Inserting the Date   *p. 68*

4 Draw a line. This line uses the 3/4-point line style. See this task:

Adding a Line to a Paragraph   *p. 144*

5 Type the memo contents.

6 Save and print the memo. See these tasks on saving and printing:

Saving a Document   *p. 90*

Printing the Document   *p. 199*

Part IX: Sample Documents

Changing the Font, p. 112

Changing the Font Size, p. 114

Inserting the Date, p. 68

Aligning Text Flush Right, p. 118

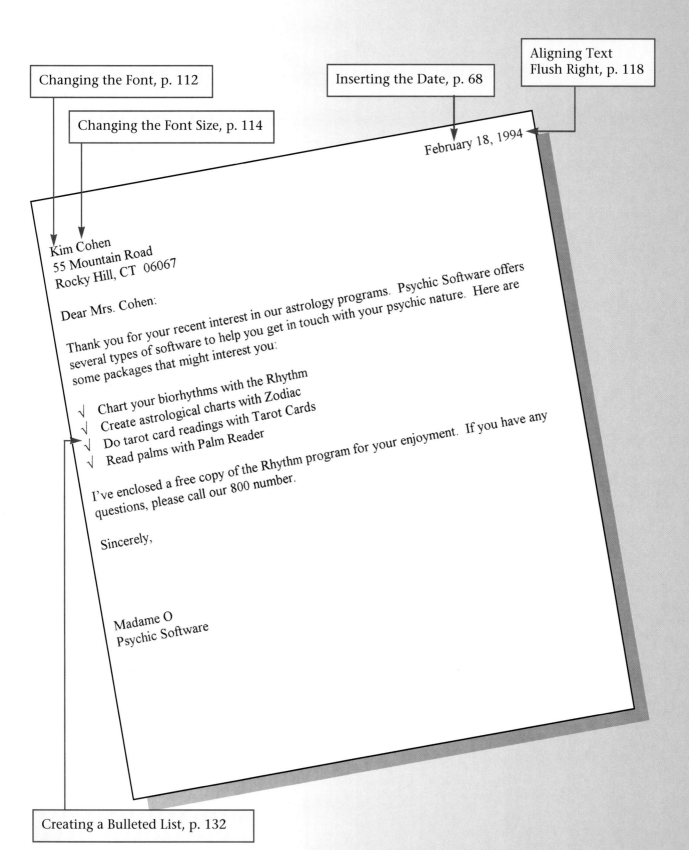

February 18, 1994

Kim Cohen
55 Mountain Road
Rocky Hill, CT 06067

Dear Mrs. Cohen:

Thank you for your recent interest in our astrology programs. Psychic Software offers several types of software to help you get in touch with your psychic nature. Here are some packages that might interest you:

√ Chart your biorhythms with the Rhythm
√ Create astrological charts with Zodiac
√ Do tarot card readings with Tarot Cards
√ Read palms with Palm Reader

I've enclosed a free copy of the Rhythm program for your enjoyment. If you have any questions, please call our 800 number.

Sincerely,

Madame O
Psychic Software

Creating a Bulleted List, p. 132

Create a business letter

1 Insert and right-align the date. These tasks explain how to complete this step:

Aligning Text Flush Right   *p. 118*

Inserting the Date   *p. 68*

2 Type the letter. The font used in this letter is Times New Roman, 12 point. You may need to change the font. Create the bulleted list in the letter. See these tasks:

Changing the Font   *p. 112*

Changing the Font Size   *p. 114*

Creating a Bulleted List   *p. 132*

3 Save and print the letter. See these tasks on saving and printing:

Saving a Document   *p. 90*

Printing the Document   *p. 199*

Part IX: Sample Documents

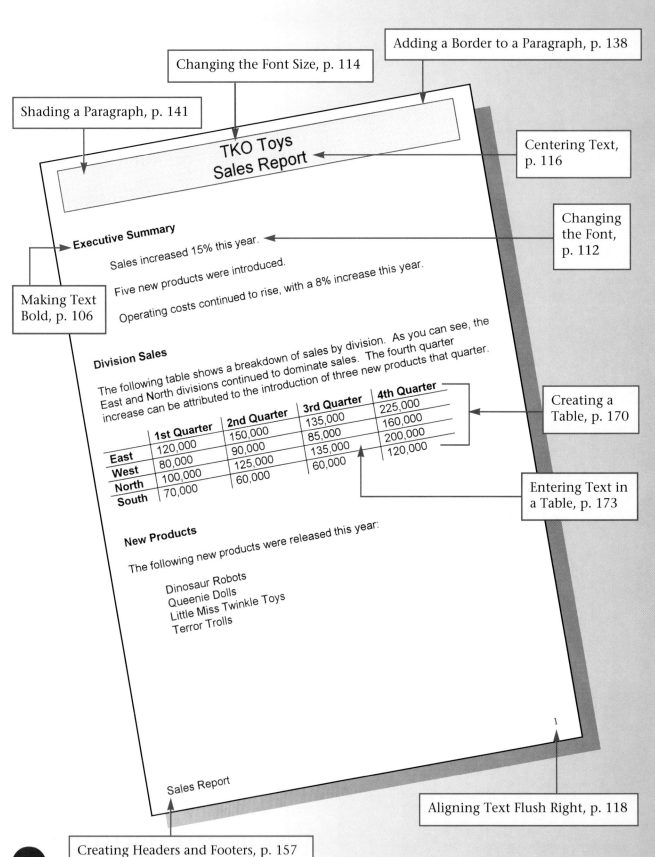

Changing the Font Size, p. 114

Adding a Border to a Paragraph, p. 138

Shading a Paragraph, p. 141

TKO Toys
Sales Report

Centering Text, p. 116

Changing the Font, p. 112

Executive Summary

Sales increased 15% this year.

Five new products were introduced.

Operating costs continued to rise, with a 8% increase this year.

Making Text Bold, p. 106

Division Sales

The following table shows a breakdown of sales by division. As you can see, the East and North divisions continued to dominate sales. The fourth quarter increase can be attributed to the introduction of three new products that quarter.

Creating a Table, p. 170

	1st Quarter	2nd Quarter	3rd Quarter	4th Quarter
East	120,000	150,000	135,000	225,000
West	80,000	90,000	85,000	160,000
North	100,000	125,000	135,000	200,000
South	70,000	60,000	60,000	120,000

Entering Text in a Table, p. 173

New Products

The following new products were released this year:

Dinosaur Robots
Queenie Dolls
Little Miss Twinkle Toys
Terror Trolls

1

Sales Report

Aligning Text Flush Right, p. 118

Creating Headers and Footers, p. 157

Create a report

1 Type the report name. Then center it, make it bold, add a paragraph border, and a paragraph shade. The font used is Arial 18 point. These tasks cover how to apply the formatting changes:

Centering Text	*p. 116*
Making Text Bold	*p. 106*
Changing the Font	*p. 112*
Changing the Font Size	*p. 114*
Shading a Paragraph	*p. 141*
Adding a Border to a Paragraph	*p. 138*

2 Type the report text. The text is Arial 12-point type. The headings are bold. Don't forget the table! Here are the tasks to help with this step:

Changing the Font	*p. 112*
Changing the Font Size	*p. 114*
Making Text Bold	*p. 106*
Creating a Table	*p. 170*
Entering Text in a Table	*p. 173*

3 Add a footer with the report name and page number. The page number is right-aligned. See these tasks:

Creating Headers and Footers	*p. 157*
Aligning Text Flush Right	*p. 118*

4 Save and print the report. See these tasks on saving and printing:

Saving a Document	*p. 90*
Printing the Document	*p. 199*

Part IX: Sample Documents

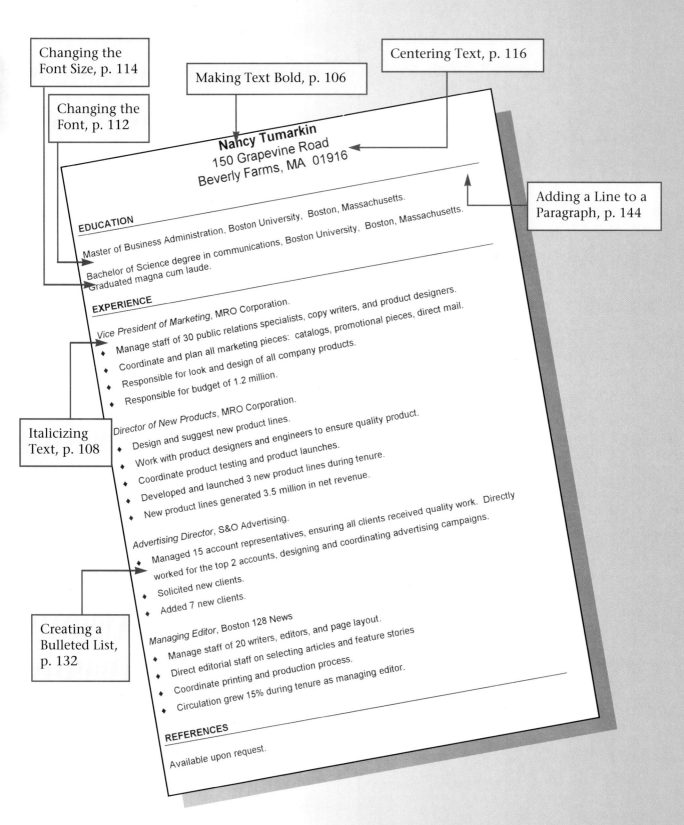

Changing the Font Size, p. 114

Changing the Font, p. 112

Making Text Bold, p. 106

Centering Text, p. 116

Adding a Line to a Paragraph, p. 144

Italicizing Text, p. 108

Creating a Bulleted List, p. 132

Nancy Tumarkin
150 Grapevine Road
Beverly Farms, MA 01916

EDUCATION

Master of Business Administration, Boston University, Boston, Massachusetts.

Bachelor of Science degree in communications, Boston University, Boston, Massachusetts.
Graduated magna cum laude.

EXPERIENCE

Vice President of Marketing, MRO Corporation.
  ♦ Manage staff of 30 public relations specialists, copy writers, and product designers.
  ♦ Coordinate and plan all marketing pieces: catalogs, promotional pieces, direct mail.
  ♦ Responsible for look and design of all company products.
  ♦ Responsible for budget of 1.2 million.

Director of New Products, MRO Corporation.
  ♦ Design and suggest new product lines.
  ♦ Work with product designers and engineers to ensure quality product.
  ♦ Coordinate product testing and product launches.
  ♦ Developed and launched 3 new product lines during tenure.
  ♦ New product lines generated 3.5 million in net revenue.

Advertising Director, S&O Advertising.
  ♦ Managed 15 account representatives, ensuring all clients received quality work. Directly worked for the top 2 accounts, designing and coordinating advertising campaigns.
  ♦ Solicited new clients.
  ♦ Added 7 new clients.

Managing Editor, Boston 128 News
  ♦ Manage staff of 20 writers, editors, and page layout.
  ♦ Direct editorial staff on selecting articles and feature stories
  ♦ Coordinate printing and production process.
  ♦ Circulation grew 15% during tenure as managing editor.

REFERENCES

Available upon request.

Create a resume

1 Type the name. The name, in this example, uses Arial 14-point type. It is centered and bold. See these tasks:

Centering Text	*p. 116*
Changing the Font	*p. 112*
Changing the Font Size	*p. 114*

2 Type the resume. Change the font to 10-point type. Make the headings bold, draw the horizontal lines, italicize the job title, and create the bulleted items, as described in these tasks:

Making Text Bold	*p. 106*
Italicizing Text	*p. 108*
Creating a Bulleted List	*p. 132*
Adding a Line to a Paragraph	*p. 144*
Changing the Font Size	*p. 144*

3 Save and print the resume. See these tasks on saving and printing:

Saving a Document	*p. 90*
Printing the Document	*p. 199*

Part IX: Sample Documents

Changing the Font, p. 112

Making Text Bold, p. 106

Changing the Font Size, p. 114

Centering Text, p. 116

Adding a Line to a Paragraph, p. 144

Inserting a Graphic, p. 162

Moving and Resizing a Graphic, p. 165

Creating Headers and Footers, p. 157

Adding a Line to a Paragraph, p. 144

Creating a Two-Column Document, p. 181

Shading a Paragraph, p. 144

Adding a Border to a Paragraph, p. 138

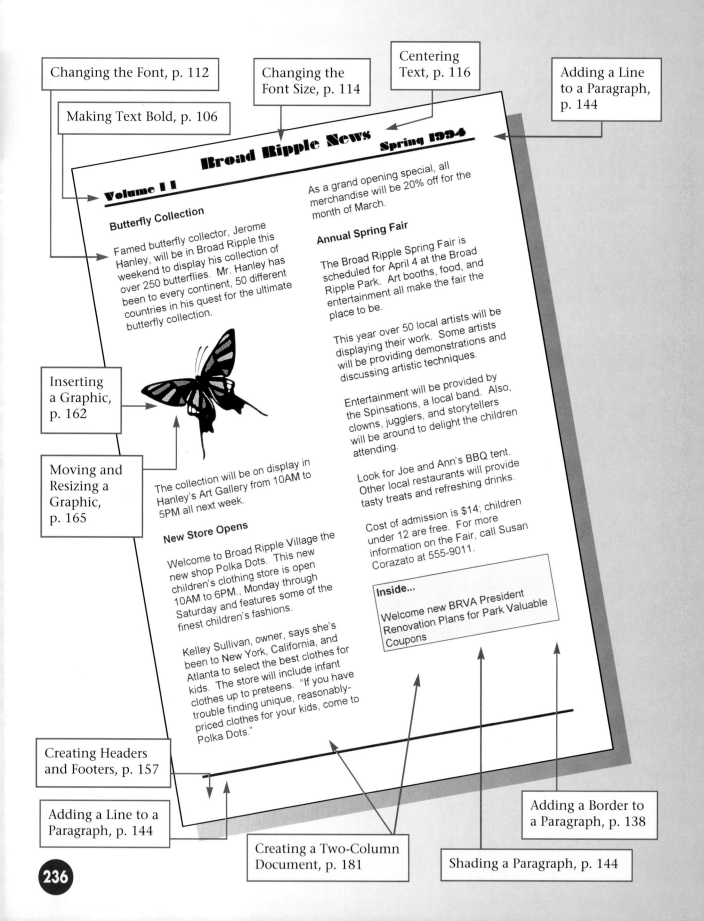

Broad Ripple News

Spring 1994

Volume 11

Butterfly Collection

Famed butterfly collector, Jerome Hanley, will be in Broad Ripple this weekend to display his collection of over 250 butterflies. Mr. Hanley has been to every continent, 50 different countries in his quest for the ultimate butterfly collection.

The collection will be on display in Hanley's Art Gallery from 10AM to 5PM all next week.

New Store Opens

Welcome to Broad Ripple Village the new shop Polka Dots. This new children's clothing store is open 10AM to 6PM., Monday through Saturday and features some of the finest children's fashions.

Kelley Sullivan, owner, says she's been to New York, California, and Atlanta to select the best clothes for kids. The store will include infant clothes up to preteens. "If you have trouble finding unique, reasonably-priced clothes for your kids, come to Polka Dots."

As a grand opening special, all merchandise will be 20% off for the month of March.

Annual Spring Fair

The Broad Ripple Spring Fair is scheduled for April 4 at the Broad Ripple Park. Art booths, food, and entertainment all make the fair the place to be.

This year over 50 local artists will be displaying their work. Some artists will be providing demonstrations and discussing artistic techniques.

Entertainment will be provided by the Spinsations, a local band. Also, clowns, jugglers, and storytellers will be around to delight the children attending.

Look for Joe and Ann's BBQ tent. Other local restaurants will provide tasty treats and refreshing drinks.

Cost of admission is $14; children under 12 are free. For more information on the Fair, call Susan Corazato at 555-9011.

Inside...

Welcome new BRVA President
Renovation Plans for Park Valuable
Coupons

Create a newsletter

1 Type the newsletter banner. The first line is centered, bold, and uses Braggadocio 16-point type. The second line uses the same font in 12-point. See these tasks for help:

Centering Text	*p. 116*
Making Text Bold	*p. 106*
Changing the Font	*p. 112*
Changing the Font Size	*p. 114*

2 Draw a line. This line uses the 3-point line style. See this task:

Adding a Line to a Paragraph	*p. 144*

3 Insert a section break, and turn on two columns. See these tasks for help:

Creating a Two-Column Document	*p. 181*

4 Format the headings. The headings are Arial 12-point type, and boldface. The article text is Arial 12-point type. The body text is set to normal. See these tasks:

Changing the Font	*p. 112*
Changing the Font Size	*p. 114*
Making Text Bold	*p. 106*

5 Shade the last section. See these tasks for help:

Adding a Border to a Paragraph	*p. 138*
Shading a Paragraph	*p. 141*

6 Insert and place the graphic. See these tasks for help:

Inserting a Graphic	*p. 162*
Moving and Resizing a Graphic	*p. 165*

7 Create a footer and insert a 3-point line in the footer. See these tasks:

Creating Headers and Footers	*p. 157*
Adding a Line to a Paragraph	*p. 144*

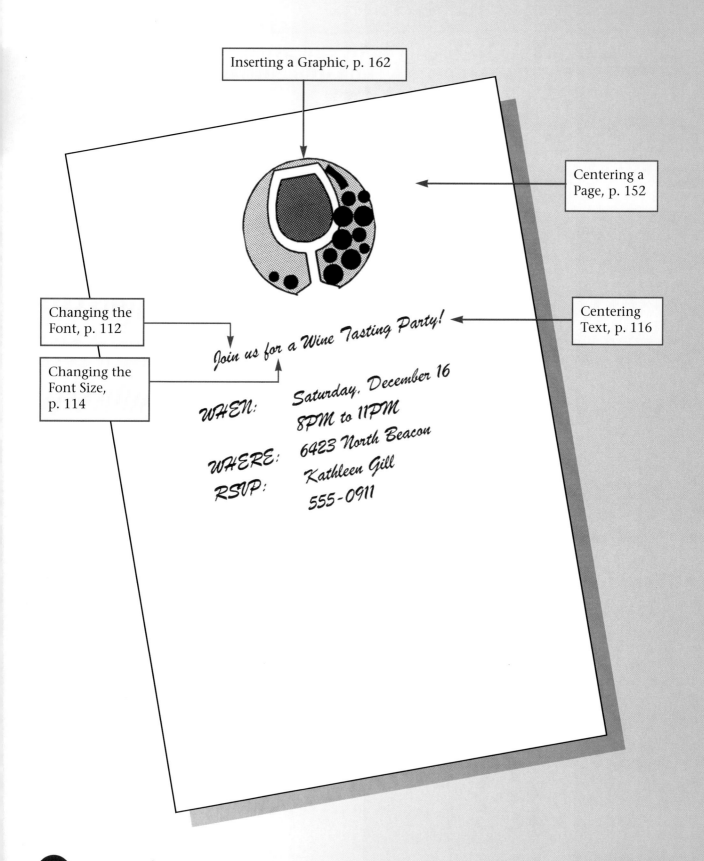

Inserting a Graphic, p. 162

Centering a Page, p. 152

Changing the Font, p. 112

Centering Text, p. 116

Changing the Font Size, p. 114

Join us for a Wine Tasting Party!

WHEN: Saturday, December 16
8PM to 11PM

WHERE: 6423 North Beacon

Kathleen Gill

RSVP: 555-0911

Create an invitation

1 Insert a graphic. This graphic uses the clip art WINE.WMF. The paragraph is centered. See this task:

Inserting a Graphic   *p. 162*

2 Type and center the heading. Indent the other lines with tabs. This text uses Brush Script MT 16-point type. See these tasks:

Centering Text   *p. 116*

Changing the Font   *p. 112*

Changing the Font Size   *p. 114*

3 Center the invitation on the page. See this task:

Centering a Page   *p. 152*

4 Save and print the invitation. See these tasks on saving and printing:

Saving a Document   *p. 90*

Printing the Document   *p. 199*

Part IX: Sample Documents

Changing the Font Size, p. 114

Centering Text, p. 116

Changing the Font, p. 112

Italicizing Text, p. 108

Indenting Text, p. 120

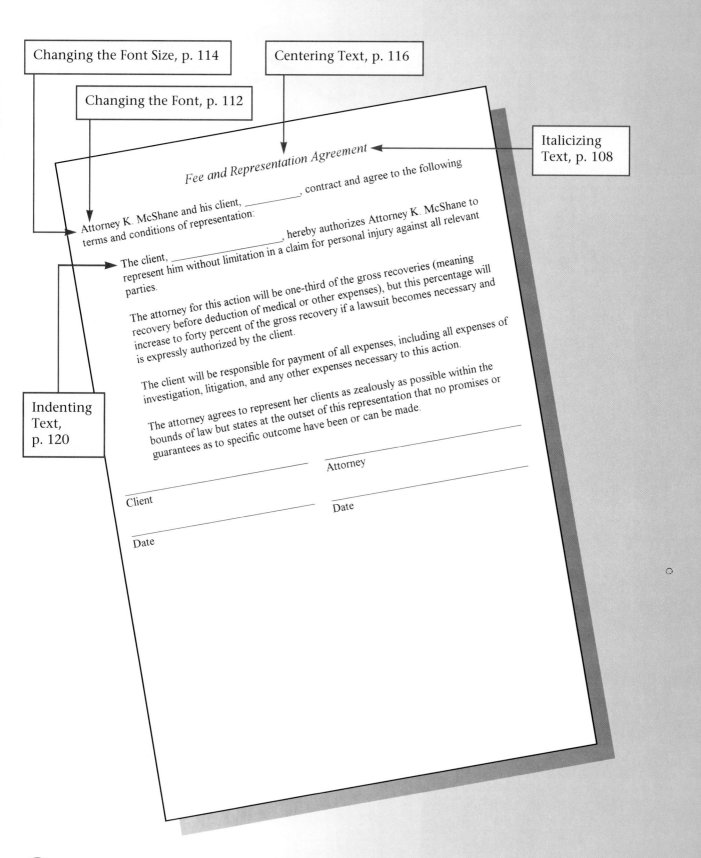

Fee and Representation Agreement

Attorney K. McShane and his client, _____, contract and agree to the following terms and conditions of representation:

The client, _____, hereby authorizes Attorney K. McShane to represent him without limitation in a claim for personal injury against all relevant parties.

The attorney for this action will be one-third of the gross recoveries (meaning recovery before deduction of medical or other expenses), but this percentage will increase to forty percent of the gross recovery if a lawsuit becomes necessary and is expressly authorized by the client.

The client will be responsible for payment of all expenses, including all expenses of investigation, litigation, and any other expenses necessary to this action.

The attorney agrees to represent her clients as zealously as possible within the bounds of law but states at the outset of this representation that no promises or guarantees as to specific outcome have been or can be made.

_____
Attorney

_____
Client

_____
Date

_____
Date

Create a contract

1 Type the heading. Make it italic and centered. This example uses Times New Roman 14-point type. See these tasks:

Italicizing Text	*p. 108*
Centering Text	*p. 116*
Changing the Font	*p. 112*
Changing the Font Size	*p. 114*

2 Type the contract. Indent the paragraphs. See this task:

Indenting Text	*p. 120*

3 Press SHIFT, then the underscore key to create blank lines.

4 Save and print the contract. See these tasks on saving and printing:

Saving a Document	*p. 90*
Printing the Document	*p. 199*

Glossary

Clipboard   A temporary storage place for text or graphics. When you cut or copy text or graphics, the program stores that item in the Clipboard. The Clipboard is a Windows feature.

Control menu box   The hyphen or box that appears at the left end of a window's title bar. Double-clicking this box closes the window.

default   Standard Word for Windows settings that are in effect each time you start the program.

dialog box   A window that displays additional command options. Many times a dialog box reminds you of the consequence or result of a command and asks you to confirm that you want to go ahead with the action.

directory   An index to the files stored on disk or a list of files. A directory is similar to a file cabinet; you can group files together in directories.

document window   The area in which you type text. You can have more than one document window open at one time.

DOS   An acronym for *disk operating system*. DOS manages the details of your system-storing and retrieving programs and files.

file   The various individual reports, memos, databases, letters, and so on that you store on your hard disk (or floppy disks) for future use. The actual Word for Windows program also is stored in a file.

file name   The name that you assign to a file when you store it to disk. A file name has two parts: the root and the extension. The root can include up to eight characters. The extension can have up to three characters, usually indicates the file type, and is optional. The root and extension are separated by a period. For example, MEMO.DOC is a valid file name. MEMO is the root, and DOC is the extension.

floppy disk drive   The door into your computer. The floppy disk drive enables you to put information onto the computer—onto the hard drive and to take information off the computer—onto a floppy disk.

font   The style, size, and typeface of a set of characters.

hard disk drive   The device within your system unit that stores the programs and files with which you work. A hard disk drive is similar to a floppy disk drive except that a hard disk holds more information, stores and retrieves information much more quickly, and usually is not removable.

hard return   A code the program inserts in the document when you press Enter. You use hard returns to end paragraphs or to insert blank lines.

icon A picture that represents a group window, an application, a document, or another element within a window.

insertion point A flashing vertical line that indicates where you will begin typing text, deleting text, selecting text, and so on.

menu An on-screen list of Word for Windows commands.

Microsoft Windows An operating environment that provides a graphical interface (rather than DOS). A graphical interface enables a user to learn a computer program more intuitively and to use a computer program more easily. You use Microsoft Windows to manage your computer system to run programs, copy files, and so on.

mouse An input device that enables you to move the insertion point, select text, select menu commands, and perform other operations.

mouse pointer The on-screen graphic that moves when you move the mouse on a flat surface. The mouse pointer appears as an arrow in menus and dialog boxes, and as an I-beam in the text area.

path name The route, through directories, to a program or document file. For example, the path name C:\WINWORD\DATA\REPORT.DOC includes these elements: the disk drive (C:), the root directory (\), the directory (WINWORD), the subdirectory (a directory within the first directory, DATA), and the file name (REPORT.DOC).

root directory The main directory. All other directories are contained in the root directory.

ruler An on-screen option bar that enables you to make formatting changes (to change tabs, indents, and margins). You can turn the display of the ruler on or off.

scroll bars The bars at the bottom and right side of a document window. At the ends of each scroll bar are scroll arrows; click any scroll arrow to scroll the window in that direction.

status bar The bottom line of the Word for Windows screen. This line displays messages, the location of the insertion point, the page number, and other information.

title bar The area of the document (or application) window that displays the name of the document (or application).

toolbar An on-screen option bar that contains buttons you can use to access commonly used commands. You can turn the display of the toolbar on or off.

window A rectangular area on-screen where you view an application or a document. A window can contain icons that represent applications, the application itself, or a document you created by using an application.

word wrap A feature that eliminates the need to press Enter each time you reach the right margin. Instead, Word for Windows "wraps" the word to the next line automatically.

Index

A–B

aligning text, 116-124
arranging windows, 89

Backspace key, 35-54
blank lines, 41-42
boldface text, 106-107
borders (paragraphs), 138-140, 144-146
bulleted lists, 132-134

C

cells (tables), 174
centering pages, 152-154
centering text, 116-117
Clipboard, 57, 242
Close command (File menu), 19, 92-93
closing documents, 88, 92-93
columns, 181-183
combining paragraphs, 43-44
commands, *see* individual commands
Contents command (Help menu), 25
control menu boxes, 242
Copy command (Edit menu), 58
copying text, 56-58
Cut command (Edit menu), 60

D

Data Form dialog box, 213-216
data sources (merges), 208-216, 223-224
Date and Time command (Insert menu), 68-70
date/time options, 66-70
default tabs, 46, 147-149
Delete Cells command (Table menu), 179

Delete key, 35, 54
deleting
    blank lines, 42
    graphics, 168-169
    merge records, 216
    rows (tables), 178-180
    text, 35, 54-55
    Wo rdArt objects, 186
dialog boxes, 12, 242
    Data Form, 213-216
    Date and Time, 69-70
    Find, 751
    Go To, 50
    How To, 26
    Insert Graphic, 163-164
    Merge, 224
    Merge Mail Helper, 207-210
    Object, 185
    Open, 99-100
    Page Numbers, 156
    Page Setup, 151
    Paragraph, 123
    Print, 200
    Replace, 78-80
    Save As, 91, 222
    Save Data Source, 211
    Spelling, 82-83
    Symbol, 67, 71-73
    Thesaurus, 85
    Tip of the Day, 15, 27-28
    Toolbars, 21
directories, 97, 246
documents, 94-95
    printing, 199-201
    sample documents, 227-241
    saving, 88-91
DOS (disk operating system), 242
double-spacing documents, 125-126
dragging/dropping text, 57

E

Edit menu commands
    Copy, 58
    Cut, 60
    Find, 75
    Go To, 49-50
    Paste, 58, 61
    Replace, 78
    Undo, 63
Exit command (File menu), 15
exiting Word, 15
Extend mode (text), 33

F

field codes, 70
File menu commands
    Close, 19, 92-93
    Exit, 15
    New, 95
    Open, 97
    Page Setup, 151-154
    Print, 200
    Save, 91
    Save As, 222
files, 242
Find command (Edit menu), 75
floppy disk drives, 242
fonts, 104, 112-115, 242
footers, *see* headers/footers
Format menu commands, 123
formatting, 104
Formatting toolbar, 13, 18

G

Go To command (Edit menu), 49-50
Graphic command (Insert menu), 163
graphics, 162-169

H

handles, 166
hanging indents, 122-124
hard disk drives, 242
hard returns, 242
Header and Footer
    command (View menu),
    158, 161
headers/footers, 157-161
Help, 24-28
Help menu commands, 25,
    27
hiding
        ruler, 22-23
        toolbars, 20-21
How To dialog box, 26

I

icons, 243
indenting text, 120-121
Insert menu commands
        Date and Time, 68-70
        Graphic, 163-164
        Object, 185
        Page Numbers, 156
        Symbol, 72
Insert mode, 34-35
Insert Rows command
    (Table menu), 177
inserting
        blank lines, 41-42
        graphics, 162-164
        merge fields, 218-220
        page breaks, 47-48
        rows (tables), 176-177
        special characters,
            71-73
        tabs, 45-46
        WordArt objects,
            184-186
insertion point, 13, 243
italic text, 108-109

K-L

keyboard shortcuts, 32-33
lists
        bulleted, 132-134
        numbered, 135-137
        tables, 170-175

M

Mail Merge command
    (Tools menu), 207, 224
mail merges, *see* merges
main documents (merges),
    206-207, 227-224
margins, 150-151
memos, 228-229
menu bar, 12
menus, 243
merges, 203-224
Microsoft Windows, 243
mouse, 25, 243
moving
        graphics, 165-167
        text, 59-61

N

navigating documents, 32,
    38-40, 49-50
New command (File
    menu), 95
newsletters, 181-183,
    238-241
numbered lists, 135-137
numbering pages, 155-156

O

Object command (Insert
    menu), 185
on-line help, 24-28
Open command (File
    menu), 97
opening documents,
    96-100
Overwrite mode, 37
overwriting text, 36-37

P-Q

page breaks, 47-48
Page Layout view, 192-193
Page Numbers command
    (Insert menu), 156
Page Setup command (File
    menu), 151-154
Paragraph command
    (Format menu), 123
paragraphs, 141-146
        borders, 138-140
        combining, 43-44
        displaying paragraph
            marks, 42
        splitting, 44
Paste command (Edit
    menu), 58, 61
path names, 243
pointer (mouse), 243
previewing documents
    (printing), 197-198
Print command (File
    menu), 200
printing, 191-201

R

removing
        page breaks, 48
        text formatting, 107
Replace command (Edit
    menu), 78
replacing text, 77-80
reports, 233-234
restoring deleted text, 55
resumes, 236-237
right-aligning text, 118-119
root directories, 243
rows (tables), 176-180
ruler, 13, 22-23, 243
Ruler command (View
    menu), 23, 148

Index

S

sample documents, 227-243
Save As command (File menu), 222
Save command (File menu), 91
Save Data Source dialog box, 211
saving, 88-91, 212-213, 221-222
scroll bars, 38-40, 243
selecting
    commands, 16-17
    text, 33, 51-53
Setup options (printing), 191
shading paragraphs, 141-143
sizing
    fonts, 114-115
    graphics, 165-167
soft page breaks, 48
special characters, 66, 71-73
spell checking, 81-83
splitting paragraphs, 44
Standard toolbar, 13, 18-19
starting Word, 14-15
status bar, 243
Symbol command (Insert menu), 72
Symbol dialog box, 67, 71-73

T

Table menu commands
    Delete Cells, 179
    Insert Rows, 177
tables, 170-180
tabs
    inserting, 45-46
    default, 147-149

thesaurus, 84-85
Thesaurus command (Tools menu), 85
tildes, 66
time/date options, 66-70
Tip of the Day command (Help menu), 27-28
Tip of the Day feature, 24, 27-28
title bar, 243
toolbars, 12-13, 18-21, 243
Toolbars command (View menu), 21
Tools menu commands
    Mail Merge, 207, 224
    Thesaurus, 85
ToolTips feature, 13
two-column documents, 181-183

U

umlauts, 66
underlined text, 110-111
Undo command (Edit menu), 63

V

View menu commands
    Header and Footer, 158, 161
    Ruler, 23, 148
    Toolbars, 21

W-Z

windows, 89, 243
wingdings, 66
word wrap, 243
WordArt objects, 184-186
zooming documents, 194-196